ATTORNEY FOR THE FRONTIER

ATTORNEY FOR THE FRONTIER

Enos Stutsman

BY DALE GIBSON

WITH LEE GIBSON AND CAMERON HARVEY

THE UNIVERSITY OF MANITOBA PRESS

© The University of Manitoba Press   1983
Printed in Canada
Designed by Norman Schmidt
This book has been published with the assistance of the Canada Council.
The frontispiece is a photograph of Enos Stutsman in 1864.

Illustrations frontispiece, 6, 9, 11, 23
courtesy of Orin G. Libby Manuscript Collection, Chester Fritz
Library, University of North Dakota

Illustration 1
courtesy of the State Historical Society, Iowa State Historical Department

Illustration 2
courtesy of Sioux City Public Museum

Illustrations 3, 4, 7
courtesy of Yankton County Historical Society

Illustrations 5, 12, 22, 25
courtesy of the State Historical Society of North Dakota

Illustrations 10, 14, 15, 16, 17, 18, 19, 20, 21
courtesy of the Provincial Archives of Manitoba

Illustration 24
courtesy of the Minnesota Historical Society

Canadian Cataloguing in Publication Data

Gibson, Dale.
  Attorney for the frontier

Includes index.
ISBN 0-88755-131-9

1. Stutsman, Enos.   2. Dakota – Biography.
3. Red River Rebellion, 1869-1870.
Cameron, 1939–   II. Gibson, Lee, 1933–
III. Title   I. Harvey,
F655.S78G528   978'.02   C83-091173-1

46, 917

CONTENTS

ACKNOWLEDGMENTS

ENOS STUTSMAN IS AN ALMOST FORGOTTEN frontier figure, remembered only by the name of a county in North Dakota, a street in Pembina, and a few fragmentary, often inaccurate, references in regional and specialist histories. The attempt to shed light on the personality and career of so elusive a person required the assistance of numerous individuals and organizations. Happily, such assistance was almost always made available – often enthusiastically – when requested. I wish to record my gratitude to all who helped, and to acknowledge explicitly some of the more important contributions.

The greatest debt is owed to Lee Gibson and Cameron Harvey. Although Lee and Cam have chosen to be designated as "assistants," they would be more accurately described as collaborators. The Stutsman project has been a shared hobby for the three of us over the past dozen or so years. The idea of undertaking a study of Stutsman occurred independently to Cam and to Lee and me at about the same time, and we agreed to join forces as soon as we learned of each others' interest. Cam carried out the bulk of the research on Stutsman's early years, shared in research for the later periods, and provided valuable criticism of the manuscript as it evolved. Lee participated in the research at several stages, offered wise advice throughout, prepared the index, organized the illustrations, and generally co-ordinated the final stages of the project. Without the efforts of Cam and Lee it is doubtful that this book would ever have been completed.

A multitude of others also helped. Mrs. A.J. Christopher of Pembina provided several useful early leads, along with coffee, cookies, and friendly encouragement. The expertise, courteous assistance, and moral support of Dan Rylance, of the Chester Fritz Library, University of North Dakota, made our visits to that institution memorable occasions. Ed Ness and Carl Wells of Sioux City were foremost among several very co-operative persons from that city. Ellen Tobin of Yankton made important contributions to our knowledge of Stutsman's Yankton years. Among our contacts in Jamestown, Mrs. Mary Young was especially helpful. And there were so many others – in the places mentioned, and in Iowa City, Des Moines, Cavalier, Pierre, Bismarck, St. Paul, and Winnipeg – that a complete list of those who helped in one way or another is just not possible. Thank you all.

Organizations that have materially assisted the project include the National Archives and Library of Congress in Washington, the Public Archives of Canada, the Provincial Archives of Manitoba, Queen's University Archives, the Department of Special Collections, Chester Fritz Library, University of North Dakota, the Minnesota State Historical Society, the Canada Council, the faculties of Law and Graduate Studies and Research of the University of Manitoba, and, of course, the University of Manitoba Press. The sensitive editorship of Carol Dahlstrom significantly improved the quality of the book.

Production of the typescript was made to look easy by the competence of several members of the Law Faculty support staff. The skill and devotion of Millicent Freeman, Agnes Dickof and Cheryl Hapko were especially appreciated. Only they and I know how much talent and effort was required to transform the scribbled, misspelled, ungrammatical copy they were handed into the typescript they produced. I hope they also know how warm my gratitude is.

The task was made much easier than it would otherwise have been by Marjorie A. Stoa, whose 1962 thesis on Stutsman blazed a trail for others to follow. Finally, to Judge Roy St. George Stubbs, who introduced us to Enos Stutsman and so much else, Lee and Cam and I offer our continuing gratitude.

Dale Gibson
Winnipeg
May, 1983

PROLOGUE

January 9, 1870

THE TERRITORY WE NOW CALL MANITOBA was in a state of insurrection. The rebel leader, Louis Riel, was being pulled in opposite directions by rival factions within his provisional government. One group urged union with the new Dominion of Canada; another called for annexation by the United States.

That evening a sled arrived in Winnipeg carrying Colonel Enos Stutsman from Pembina in the Dakota Territory. Stutsman was a familiar figure to the residents of Winnipeg, and his arrival, as envoy from those south of the international border who favored American annexation, was believed by many to be a crucial event in the contest between Canada and the United States for control of the vast prairie wilderness stretching westward to the Rocky Mountains. One of the settlement's most politically astute residents noted the event in his diary: "Mr. LeMay and Col. Stutsman arrived from Pembina today – the latter brought his traps intending to remain in the settlement for a month or two. Stutsman is up to something..."[1]

An observer not already familiar with Colonel Stutsman's

appearance would have taken notice as the gentleman climbed from his sled in front of Emmerling's Hotel. The face, though ruddy and frost-rimed from the sixty-mile midwinter trek, was fine featured and sensitive. The body was obviously powerful, but as Stutsman disentangled himself from the protective furs, he reached for a pair of short crutches, and onlookers would have observed that he had no legs. No legs to speak of, at least; in place of legs a birth defect had left him with only a small stump, an undeveloped limb that merely served as pivot for his crutches.

The story of this remarkable man – frontier lawyer, politician, journalist, land speculator, bon vivant – and how he came to be in a position to bargain for a territory larger than the Louisiana Purchase, has seldom been told.[2] It deserves a wider audience.

ATTORNEY FOR THE FRONTIER

CHAPTER ONE

SIOUX CITY AND BEFORE 1826-1858

T HE STUTSMAN FAMILY, GERMAN IN ORIGIN, had been in America for almost a century before Enos was born in 1826. Two cousins, both named Jacob Stutsman, had settled in Pennsylvania in 1728, founding two branches of the family. In a newspaper sketch of 1862, Enos claimed that members of both branches had participated in most of the major military struggles in American history – the War for Independence, the War of 1812, the Blackhawk War, the Mexican War – and were, at the time the sketch was published, fighting on both sides of the Civil War.[1]

The family seems to have had a considerable wanderlust. The southern branch was established when one of the original cousins moved to North Carolina. The other cousin remained in Pennsylvania, but his son, Enos's grandfather, moved westward, to the present site of Dayton, Ohio in 1779. Enos's father, Nicholas, moved on in his turn to Fayette County, Indiana, where Enos was born on February 14, 1826,[2] and then again, ten years later, to Coles County, Illinois, not far from the farm of Abraham Lincoln's father. This family trait may account in part for the restlessness and love of frontier life later to be exhibited by Enos. However, in view of his disability there must also have been some other, more compelling, motivation to be always at the point where civilization and wilderness meshed.

The anguish of childhood for someone as severely disabled as Enos Stutsman can readily be imagined. The fact that his family lived in a very remote area during his earliest years no doubt compounded his difficulties. Although he was blessed with an unusually quick mind, and might be expected to compensate for his physical shortcomings by following intellectual pursuits, he was apparently unable to attend school until the age of ten, when his family moved to Illinois. Nevertheless, a remarkably sunny disposition throughout his adult life (punctuated, it is true, by occasional storms of impulsive anger) testifies to the likelihood that he grew up in a loving and happy home.

When the opportunity for schooling finally arrived, Enos made the most of it. By the age of seventeen he was judged well enough educated to be employed as a teacher himself, a position he held for four years. Although he never displayed the acquaintance with classical history and literature that contemporaries educated in eastern schools and universities could boast, and his spelling was often faulty, Stutsman's frontier education equipped him with an impressive command of the English language, a wide range of general knowledge, and a thirst for further learning. These qualities, added to a keen intelligence, insured that he would have little to fear from anyone in intellectual combat.

As he approached adulthood, Enos displayed other important assets. He seems to have enjoyed robust health; he certainly possessed extraordinary vitality. Although his disability deprived him of normal locomotion, he could move about with surprising speed on short crutches. Observers marvelled at his ability to vault into a saddle or a wagon seat.

Perhaps his most valuable asset was his personality. For one who had grown up largely house-bound in a remote part of the American northwest, Enos was astonishingly outgoing and socially assured. His photographs betray a certain sensitivity, and accounts by those who knew him reveal occasional bouts of moodiness and anger, but these are hardly surprising in view of the disadvantage under which he constantly labored. What is remarkable is how seldom he permitted these characteristics to prevail over his customary conviviality and charm, and how consistent was his rich, often mischievous, sense of humor. These personality traits proved to be great social equalizers, and he attracted a large circle of friends. Although some of the compliments he paid to persons of influence may appear obsequious to modern eyes, he had a reputation for sincerity, and he certainly had no fear of expressing criticism or unpopular ideas when so moved.

Since vitality, intelligence, articulateness and charm are qualities highly prized in politicians, the young Enos Stutsman was unusually well endowed for public life, and he lost little time entering the forum. In 1847, toward the end of his fourth year of teaching, he reached the age of legal majority, twenty-one, and turned almost immediately to politics. He ran, as a Democrat, for the office of recorder of Coles County, and won. During the two years he held that office he began to study law, and in 1849 he sought election to a law-related position, clerk of the county court. Again he was successful. He continued his legal studies, and in 1851, at the expiration of his second term as court clerk, he was called to the Illinois bar.

Little is known about the next five years. Presumably Stutsman engaged in the private practice of law and probably in related business matters in Illinois. In 1855 he moved to Des Moines, Iowa, which was then in the midst of a land rush, and set up a real estate and banking business.[3] These ventures appear to have been successful, since Stutsman seems to have taken considerable capital with him when he made his next move, a year later, to Sioux City, Iowa.[4]

Sioux City in 1856 has been described as "a settlement of a few log huts," and as "the outer limits of civilization in the Northwest."[5] It was on the brink of a boom, however. Homesteaders were being attracted in large numbers to the rich agricultural land of the region following the land survey of 1852-55. Tradesmen of all varieties, anxious to service the new settlers, were flocking to the little town established by the Sioux City Company of survey director, Dr. J.K. Cook. The opportunity for land speculation was tempting, and Enos Stutsman decided to seize it. He sold his Des Moines interests, and was soon at the center of the Sioux City boom, hobbling energetically from one business deal to another amid the frenzy of settlers' wagons and new construction.

A newspaper advertisement that Stutsman began to run the following year gives some idea of the diversity of his business:

E. Stutsman and Co., Dealers in Real Estate... Will give their personal attention to all business entrusted to them pertaining to a general land agency and collection office. Money loaned at western rates of interest or invested in real estate. Land warrants bought and sold for cash and on time or located on government land in the Sioux, Council Bluffs, Omaha and Dakota Districts. Collection done and monies promptly remitted. Letters of inquiry or on business will be answered by return mail. A few choice tracts of land and town lots now on hand and for sale.[6]

Business was excellent. Within a short time Stutsman owned considerable property in and around Sioux City, including the building used by the City Council.[7] When he completed construction of what was described in advertisements as his "Banking House and Real Estate Agency"[8] in the late summer of 1857, a newspaper account described it as "one of the finest, if not *the* finest office in Sioux City," and added: "We trust he may make another fortune in it to add to the one that he already possesses."[9]

The joy that Stutsman seemed to derive from these intensely active and successful early days in Sioux City is conveyed by an anecdote related years later by a woman who knew him at the time:

One late afternoon it was raining. Mrs. Hittle sat on a doorstep, her husband just behind her. The bell at the Sioux City House clanged, calling the boarders to their suppers. A group of young men went hurrying by, finally breaking into a run, eager to be among the first to sit down at the table, and to get in out of the rain. Away in the rear came Stutsman on his little short crutches.

"Poor Stuts," Mrs. Hittle remarked to her husband, "He must feel badly when they go ahead and leave him like that!"

Almost before she ceased speaking, Stutsman threw back his head and began to sing his loudest, and hobbled on as fast as he could, singing in the rain.[10]

As if his real estate and banking enterprises were not keeping him busy enough, Stutsman decided to resume the practice of law. On

1. Sioux City in 1856

December 10, 1857, he was enrolled as an attorney of the Iowa Seventh District Court on the motion of John Currier, a young lawyer with whom Stutsman subsequently entered into a law partnership.[11] On January 16, 1858, the *Sioux City Iowa Eagle* announced:

> It will be seen by reference to our advertising column that E. Stutsman, Esq., and John Currier, Esq., have formed a copartnership in law business. The legal talents of these gentlemen as lawyers are already so well known that anything we might say could not add to their already well-earned reputation. We hope their cases may be many and their cause triumphant.

The accompanying advertisement (which, incidentally, indicated that Stutsman was the senior partner), included an impressive list of references for each man – the names of apparently prominent individuals in New York, Wisconsin, Illinois, Ohio, Missouri, Pennsylvania, New Hampshire, and Massachusetts. Although there is no direct evidence that these references were spurious, the likelihood of two young frontier lawyers being so well connected is not sufficiently high to overcome the suspicion that a certain amount of "puffing" was involved.

The law office of Stutsman and Currier was across the street from Stutsman's new bank building, which he sold at about this time. Both he and his partner continued to maintain separate real estate and financial operations, however, independent of the law partnership. In Stutsman's case, at least, these commercial transactions seem to have engaged at least as much of his attention as professional matters did. The records of the local district court for the period indicate that Stutsman was before the court more frequently as litigant in a variety of commercial disputes than he was in the capacity of attorney.[12]

We do know, however, that he appeared as counsel in at least one local *cause célèbre*.[13] Among those who came to Sioux City during these hectic times to offer their services to the new settlers was one Elizabeth Smith, who was arraigned on February 18, 1858, together with two male colleagues, on a charge of keeping a house of ill-fame. Stutsman and his partner represented the defendants. Employing a tactic that criminal lawyers still find useful, Stutsman requested separate trials for each defendant. The prosecuting attorney, perhaps unwisely, elected to try Elizabeth Smith first. The approach that Stutsman and Currier decided to take during the hard-fought trial was to attack the veracity of the key prosecution witness. They went beyond mere cross-examination of the witness, and actually called other witnesses to testify as to his reputation for untruthfulness. Although the state brought rebuttal evidence on the question, the defence had sown seeds of reasonable doubt in the minds of the jurors. There may also have been an element of sympathy toward a young woman standing alone against the stern power of the state. At any rate, the jury acquitted Elizabeth Smith, after lengthy debate, at 9:00 o'clock that evening. When the cases against the male defendants were proceeded with, the prosecution's case had been considerably weakened by the first acquittal, and the jury was unable to agree on a verdict. New trials were ordered, in which both men were eventually acquitted. Although he could not have had much experience in such matters at this point of his career, Stutsman appears to have become a competent courtroom lawyer.

There was time for play as well as for work. Enos had a robust appetite for the pleasures of life – for good food and drink, for companionship, for laughter and song – which he generously indulged. The *Sioux City Iowa Eagle* for November 28, 1857, records a memorable Thanksgiving Day dinner:

...at about three o'clock in the afternoon a goodly number, including many of the first men of the City, sat down together at the Tremont House, where a bountiful repast had been provided by the worthy landlord... The table had groaned with the abundance of good things... After the wants of the inner man had been supplied and the dishes removed, toasts, sentiments, speeches and songs came next in order, which were entered into with great zest, and fun and merriment went round the board... In reply to a toast for Indiana, E. Stutsman, Esq., replied in a manner popularly his own, and the building shook from foundation to rafters with prolonged cheers.

After a demonstration of the extravagant eloquence fashionable at the time, Stutsman entertained the gathering with songs. Several biographical sketches mention both his fine singing voice and his prowess as a whistler.

2. John H. Charles

John H. Charles, a fellow lawyer and close friend of Stutsman's[14] (who, by the way, had been present at the above-mentioned Thanksgiving dinner, and recalled years later seeing the guests dancing on the table), told of another incident that underlines Stutsman's sense of fun. Charles had once been a justice of the peace. On New Year's Day, 1858, he was approached by a group of Indian and Métis[15] men to perform a marriage ceremony between an Indian woman and a French-speaking Métis man across the river in the Dakota Territory. It seems that the woman had been deceived on a previous occasion, and was now insisting on a "legal" ceremony. Charles objected that he no longer had authority to perform marriages in Iowa, and had never had such authority for Dakota. The delegation insisted, however, in a somewhat menacing manner, and he eventually agreed to comply. When he did so, the following day, Enos Stutsman accompanied him. Arriving at the hut where the service was to be conducted, they discovered that the groom could not understand English, and that the bride could understand neither English nor French. Charles nevertheless carried out the marriage ritual, and pronounced the couple husband and wife. Then, perhaps sensing that the ceremony-conscious Sioux had not been fully satisfied by the rather perfunctory service, he called upon Stutsman to give an address:

This he did, giving the newly married couple some good advice (which they could not understand) and wishing all present a good time and finally that all might go to the happy hunting grounds and have a continued good time there.[16]

Another account of the same event refers to a small misfortune that befell Stutsman on the way to the ceremony, and almost prevented his participation. It offers a glimpse of the sensitivity that he normally hid from view. When the party arrived at the Indian village it was discovered that his crutches had fallen out of the wagon somewhere along the way. Another member of the group recorded Stutsman's reaction:

(W)hen he found that his aids to locomotion were gone he lapsed into a morose and sullen mood, would not accept proffered aid, threw himself upon the bottom of the wagon and pulled a robe over him and rejected all offers of assistance. Finally a pair of roughly made crutches were offered to him... At first he refused to accept them, but later, realizing the situation, he took them, threw the robe to one side, sprang out of the wagon, which he could do with the quickness and agility of a normal person, and for the balance of the night contributed his full share to the jollity of the occasion.[17]

John Charles was also a political colleague of Stutsman's. Both men were elected to the Sioux City Council at the city's first election in August 1857, but the vote was annulled by a court order,[18] apparently because the State Legislature had not yet authorized an election to be held.[19] Although Stutsman remained politically active, being appointed to the newly formed Woodbury County Central Democratic Committee in April 1858,[20] he does not seem to have been a candidate in the new election held that month.[21] The reason may well have been the fact that his financial empire was beginning to crumble.

The land boom had brought inflation to Sioux City and other settlements of the western frontier, leaving speculators like Stutsman vulnerable to an economic downturn. When the national depression of 1857 struck, it hit these communities especially hard. Stutsman, like many others, was overextended, and was unable to meet his outstanding obligations. This may be the reason he turned to the practice of law and reduced his banking activities early in 1858. He sold his grand new bank building[22] and before long he was forced to divest himself of all his other Sioux City holdings.[23]

This sudden shift in his fortunes does not seem to have dampened Stutsman's spirits. He wound up his business affairs in Sioux City, terminated his law partnership with John Currier,[24] and moved optimistically westward again, this time to a wilderness location in the Indian territories.

CHAPTER TWO

YANKTON

1859-1866

THE STORY OF STUTSMAN'S YANKTON YEARS begins with the adventures of another colorful territorial figure: Captain J.B.S. Todd. A West Point graduate, Todd came to the area first in 1855 as an officer with a military expedition dispatched to punish Indian bands that had attacked westbound overland trekkers and freight carriers. After arbitrarily butchering the first Indian band they came upon, and subsequently failing to find any others, the expedition established Fort Randall, on the Missouri River, in early 1856, to provide future protection for travellers in that part of the Indian territories.[1] Sensing an opportunity to profit from trade with the Indians, and perhaps from future land speculation, Todd obtained a leave of absence from the army (and later resigned his appointment altogether) in order to enter a trading partnership. His partner was D.M. Frost, another former military man, with whom Todd had served in the Mexican War, and who was already operating a chain of trading posts. The headquarters of the new partnership was established in Sioux City, and Todd lost no time becoming active in Sioux City affairs. He was chosen mayor in the abortive civic election of August 1857.[2] His association with Enos Stutsman dates at least from that time.

Frost, Todd and Company established a small trading post that summer at an Indian village on the Missouri where Yankton now stands. Captain Todd had his eye on more than mercantile profits. The Indian band controlled a large wilderness area with great agricultural and settlement potential. If the Indians could be induced to cede the land to the whites and move further west, there were large sums of money to be made by shrewd businessmen who were on the scene early. The problem was that the Indians were not interested in selling. An emissary sent from Washington to discuss the matter with the chiefs that summer had come away completely empty-handed.[3]

Todd thought he could succeed where others had failed. By exploiting connections he had in political circles, he managed to obtain a mandate to negotiate with the native leaders. After lengthy discussions he succeeded, in the closing months of 1857, in reaching a tentative agreement with the Indian representatives. The key to success was his decision to recruit as a colleague in the bargaining process a Métis by the name of Charles Picotte, one of the few persons born in the area who could boast a formal education. Without Picotte's involvement as translator and trusted intermediary, the negotiations would probably not have borne fruit. In December 1857 Todd and Picotte accompanied about a dozen Indian chiefs to Washington to finalize the agreement. The Indian delegation was not homogenous in opinion. The principal chief, Strike-the-Ree, favored ceding the land but Smutty Bear, a very influential subordinate leader, was highly skeptical. The dissidents were eventually won over, however, and a treaty was signed by all chiefs in April 1858. The arts of persuasion practiced on these unsophisticated wilderness people during their three-month sojourn in the nation's capital are probably best left to the imagination.

The treaty recognized the existing rights of resident Métis and provided for a large special land grant to negotiator Charles Picotte. Captain Todd's reward came in the form of a stipulation, undoubtedly included at his instigation, that:

3. J.B.S. Todd

... all other persons (other than Indians, or mixed bloods) who are now residing within the said ceded country, by authority of law, shall have the privilege of entering 160 acres thereof, to include each of their residences and improvements, at the rate of $1.25 per acre.[4]

This gave Frost, Todd and Company, with occupied trading posts at Yankton and other locations in the ceded territory, an option on extensive land, much of which had townsite potential. While the Washington negotiations were still in progress, Todd returned to Sioux City. There, in February 1858, he and Frost, together with several other speculators, formed the Upper Missouri Land Company to exploit this advantage. Enos Stutsman was designated secretary and executive officer of the company.[5]

There is some doubt as to exactly when Stutsman moved to the Yankton encampment to take up his new duties. A biographical sketch that was probably based on an interview with him claims that he "took up his residence" at Yankton in 1858,[6] and a distinguished historian refers to his supervision of a townsite survey there in the fall of that year.[7] Other sources state that he came to Yankton in 1859,[8] however, and his Sioux City law practice and real estate business continued to be advertised until June of the latter year. The best explanation of these discrepancies is probably that Stutsman visited Yankton in the summer or fall of 1858, and then returned to Sioux City for the winter.

Although the Indian treaty was not ratified by the Senate until February 1859, it is very difficult to believe that the executive officer of the newly formed land company would have been content to await that event passively. For one thing, a considerable number of rival claimants were poised on the other side of the Missouri River. Some had attempted to occupy choice sites in the cession territory as early as March 1858, and they continued to do so sporadically throughout that summer. These premature claimants had all been expelled, either by the Indians or by troops from Fort Randall, but they were ready to return at the first opportunity. Representatives of Frost, Todd and Company were permitted to remain within the territory because of their role as licenced traders (and perhaps also because of Todd's influence with the military personnel as a former officer and the current provisioner of the Fort Randall garrison.)[9] It is inconceivable that Stutsman and his colleagues would have failed to take advantage of this privileged position by staking out their claims and planning their subdivisions as soon as possible. Even if company business had not required his presence, it is highly unlikely that a man as astute as Enos Stutsman would have passed up the opportunity to establish residence in order to qualify for a personal land claim under the "prior resident" provision of the treaty. The reports that Stutsman was in Yankton to supervise surveying by at least the fall of 1858, therefore, have the ring of truth. But with the survey work completed, and winter coming on, it is not unlikely that he left the Indian camp and returned to the more convivial surroundings of Sioux City until spring.

Stutsman was undoubtedly back in Yankton well before April 19, 1859, the anniversary of the signing of the Indian treaty. The anniversary was significant because the treaty gave the Indians a year in which to move from the ceded territory to the new reservation, and the land-hungry rivals across the river in Nebraska could be expected to flock in as soon as the year was up. It was important to be on hand in advance of the invasion to forestall claim-jumping.

When he arrived, the situation was more complicated and more tense than had been expected. The Indians, more than 2,000 strong, were still encamped at Yankton, and showed no inclination to move in the near future. They interpreted the treaty as giving them a year *from the date of Senate ratification* in which to complete the move. The army did not support this quite plausible interpretation, however. The Indians, whose suspicions had already been stirred by the anticipatory surveying activities of the previous fall, were accordingly in a hostile mood. Smutty Bear was again organizing opposition to the treaty among his followers, and treaty repudiation, together with violent confrontation between whites and Indians, was a real danger. Equally disturbing was the possibility that the bitterly divided factions within the Indian community would take up arms against each other and, inevitably, draw the handful of whites on the scene into the bloodshed. Enos Stutsman and a Frost, Todd and Company

4. Strike-the-Ree (seated left), Medicine Cow (standing left), and Charles Picotte (standing center)

employee called J.S. Presho, who were living at the company's trading post, were closer to the danger than any other whites.

At the end of the first week of July the Indian leaders seemed to arrive at a peaceful resolution of their differences. The old chief, Strike-the-Ree, appeared to have convinced Smutty Bear and his dissidents to abide by the treaty, and a sumptuous feast was held to celebrate the accord. Nevertheless, the atmosphere continued to be charged with tension. An eye-witness described the situation as follows:

Medicine Cow was the military chief of the tribe, and declared martial law in the Indian village, and posted his faithful sentinels around the outlines of the whole encampment. This was done to avoid any sudden alarm or attack from the lower bands, who, in turn, enjoined the same rigid military vigilance; for the two divisions of the tribe were still suspicious of each other, even after their council and feast. Stutsman and Presho, then occupants of the "old rancho" (the Frost-Todd post), thinking their situation a little precarious, held a council of war among themselves as to the policy of fleeing or fighting, in case of attack, and finally concluded that they would stand and fight the whole Yankton tribe rather than cross the river and travel on foot to Sioux City. Finally, Strike-the-Ree placed a guard around the house and quieted their apprehensions by ordering half a dozen warriors to sleep upon the roof.[10]

Relief came a few days later, in the form of the steamboat *Carrier*. The boat arrived at the village on July 10, laden with treaty goods – the first year's installment of food, clothing, tools and money to be distributed to Strike-the-Ree's people in accordance with the treaty. Indian agent A.H. Redfield overcame the Indians' lingering reluctance to move immediately to the designated reservation by a simple but effective stratagem. He distributed a few trinkets and then announced that the bulk of the goods would be issued at the reservation site. As the steamer backed out into the river and swung into the current to resume its upstream voyage, the Indians began to break camp. Before long, most were on the Fort Randall military road, trudging toward a newly confined homeland and an uncertain future.[11] Symbolic of the significance of the migration was the solemn burial of two deceased compatriots who had previously been laid out in the open air in accordance with tribal custom.[12]

Another parting ritual must have led Stutsman to wonder whether the peace pact of the previous week had suddenly been sundered. A sizable group of mounted warriors, painted and armed, galloped furiously through the encampment waving their weapons and shouting menacingly. Fortunately, they disappeared as quickly as they had come. Startled observers concluded that the foray had merely been a final gesture of defiance and frustration by members of the dissident group.[13] Yankton now belonged to the whites.

The influx of white settlers which followed on the heels of the withdrawing natives had surprisingly little immediate effect on Yankton. There was plenty of land available in other parts of the ceded territory, and most of the initial newcomers headed for sites they could claim as their own rather than for the proposed Yankton townsite, where they would have to buy from the Frost–Todd group. The most populous new settlement near Yankton sprang up along the James River, several miles to the east, where Vermillion now stands. In October 1859, three months after the Indians had left, there were still only two buildings on the site of their former camp: the original Frost–Todd trading post, where Stutsman and his cronies lived, and a cabin built by Charles Picotte on his treaty tract. Two other structures were completed by the following spring, however: an inn operated by Henry Ash and his wife, and a general store built by a gentleman with the improbable name of Downer T. Bramble. Construction of these early buildings was no easy matter; as there was no suitable timber available in the vicinity, building supplies had to be transported from a distance.[14]

As winter set in, prospects must have appeared rather bleak to the handful of settlers at Yankton and the slightly larger cluster of James River homesteaders. Their hastily constructed dwellings were cramped and cold, and their inability to plant crops that first year, due to the delayed withdrawal of the Indians, had left them with only rudimentary food supplies. Mary Ash, the wife of the new innkeeper, arrived in Yankton with her three children the day before Christmas. After a simple supper in the rude temporary quarters Henry Ash had just completed, there was a small Christmas Eve party at the trading post. One of the Ash children recalled the event:

After supper father, mother and myself went to Presho's cabin to spend Christmas eve, who we found boiling mush in an old black kettle. As party guests were D.T. Bramble, Stutsman, Charley Picotte, father, mother, myself and Hadway, an Indian highly educated in St. Louis who lived with his wife, an Indian woman, at the mouth of the Rhine creek... Presho filled some tin plates for each one of us with blackstrap molasses as sugar. It made a real Christmas treat. I lapped up my dish of mush in a few minutes.[15]

Fortunately, the fabled Missouri River catfish were plentiful. J.J. Audubon, the pioneer naturalist, had recently studied the species, and had pronounced it to be a very valuable food source.[16] The Yankton area homesteaders needed no scholarly urging to exploit fully the nutritional and gastronomic bonanza that nature had placed at their doorsteps. Whether or not the reports of numerous fish in the 200- and 300-pound range were accurate,[17] there is little doubt that Big Muddy cats were both the staple and the luxury of most pioneer diets in the early years.

There was plenty of time during that first uneventful winter to follow the tumult of the outside world through newspapers, and to daydream of a time when the former Indian village and its new inhabitants would play a significant role in the business and political affairs of the nation. Enos Stutsman appears to have taken full advantage of this opportunity for study and reflection. A letter to the editor of a Sioux City newspaper, written January 2, 1860 by an anonymous Yankton resident, most likely Stutsman himself, described the periodicals regularly perused:

The Daily Missouri Republican, The Tri-Weekly Missouri Republican, The Weekly Missouri Republican, The Weekly (Philadelphia) Press, The New York Times, The New York Herald, The New York Tribune, The Weekly (Wash.) Constitution, The St. Louis Bulletin, The St. Joseph Journal, Charleston (S. C.) Mercury, Daily St. Joseph Gazette, Cleveland Morning Journal, Newark Weekly Journal, Wisconsin Daily State Journal, Glen's Falls (N. Y.) Messenger, Lewis County (N. Y.) Banner, Ellenville (N. Y.) Journal, Chenango (N. Y.) American, Chenango (N. Y.) Union, Montreal Gazette, Natchez Daily Courier, Springfield (Mass.) Republican, Chicago Weekly Times, Cincinatti Dollar Times, Sioux City Register, Council Bluffs Bugle, Iowa State Journal, Iowa State Reporter, Cedar Valley Times, Ft. Dodge Sentinel, Germantown (Pa.) Telegraph, Bucks County (Pa.) Intelligencer, American Messenger and six choice Magazines.[18]

The writer felt compelled to add that although the journals listed displayed a catholicity of political outlook, the four gentlemen listed were all "sound Democrats."

The main purpose of the letter was doubtless to attract the attention of potential immigrants to the new community, and some of the hyperbole indulged in must have provoked chuckles among readers familiar with the actual conditions in the tiny settlement:

Yancton (sic) is improving steadily, and what promises a future healthy growth for our young city, is, that the surrounding country is rapidly filling up with substantial farmers. This exceedingly pleasant winter is peculiarly favorable to emigration and improvements, so that, by the opening of navigation you will be astonished to observe the almost magical change in the business and appearance of Yancton, Vermillion and indeed the entire country skirting the east bank of the Missouri River...

When the decennial census was taken the next summer, a much less expansive picture emerged. There were only about 500 permanent white settlers on the entire Missouri slope,[19] fewer than half of whom would have been located in the vicinity of Yankton. The same census tells us that Enos Stutsman, 34 years of age, lawyer by occupation, delcared a total personal worth of $600: $400 in real property holdings, and $200 in personal property.[20] The tides of fortune had clearly ebbed for the former Sioux City tycoon.

He was far from defeated, however. Animated by his customary optimism, he moved about the tiny community, passing the time of day with friends, watching such construction as there was, greeting occasional newcomers, and chatting with the passengers and crew of passing riverboats – vigilant for opportunities, large or small, to turn his talents to profit. Although the census disclosed that eight residents of the Territory described themselves as lawyers,[21] Stutsman was the only legally trained person at Yankton, and he undoubtedly received occasional calls for professional services.

The only recorded instance of his practicing law that year occurred in March, when a dispute arose between competing claimants for the ownership of certain land in the nearby Smutty Bear Bottom. Because the Territory still lacked a governmental structure, there was no legal mechanism available for the adjudication of such disputes. The parties agreed, therefore, to submit their differences to an informal jury of six local residents. The trial was held in Downer Bramble's store. Enos Stutsman acted as lawyer for one party – a former employee of Frost, Todd and Company, called William Lyman, who had been present in the village as trader even before the Indian treaty was signed. Lyman won. Whether the victory was attributable to the righteousness of his claim, to Stutsman's eloquence, or to the fact that Stutsman's cabin-mate, J.S. Presho, was on the jury, is unknown.[22]

In 1861 the tempo of events accelerated, at least on the political front. The absence of satisfactory governmental machinery at the time the ceded territory was first opened to settlement had been the result of several coinciding factors. The area had been a part of the Minnesota Territory prior to 1858, but when the State of Minnesota was created that year its boundaries were smaller than those of the Territory had been, and did not encompass the land involved in the cession treaty. Doubt prevailed as to whether the laws and political arrangements of the former Territory still applied to the cession lands. If they did, nothing was done to put them into operation. Much of the blame for this can probably be attributed to the fact that the rest of the nation was preoccupied with the looming civil war; the question of governmental arrangements for a few hundred denizens of the northwestern wilderness had low priority. Even for those few politicians who were interested in the question, there was a sub-issue that presented a stubborn impediment to progress: whether the new territory should be constitutionally committed to an anti-slavery policy. Moreover, Washington was receiving inconsistent advice from various factions within the territory as to the most suitable form of political organization.

When the logjam finally broke, early in 1861, it seems to have been due largely to the patient and effective lobbying of Captain J.B.S. Todd. In the fall of 1859, Todd and his partner, Frost, had circulated a petition among the settlers calling for prompt congressional action. Todd had delivered the petition to Washington in person, but without success. After the election of Abraham Lincoln to the presidency, Todd renewed the campaign, assisted by another memorial drawn up by the settlers in January 1861. Although he was a Democrat, Todd seems to have had considerable influence with Lincoln, perhaps because he was a native of Springfield, Illinois, and was a cousin of Lincoln's wife. Lincoln seems to have given the word to proceed with the territorial legislation. In February, the Republican group in Congress that had been demanding an anti-slavery provision in the organizational legislation suddenly dropped the requirement, and the bill creating the Dakota Territory was passed without debate. President Buchanan signed the measure on March 2, 1861, two days before Lincoln's inauguration. A Yankton resident recorded that when the news reached the settlement eleven days later "hats, hurrahs and town lots 'went up' to greet the dawning future of the great northwest."[23]

John Todd fully expected to be named first governor of the Dakota Territory. And for good reason: no one had done more than he to bring the Territory into existence. Unfortunately, his partner Daniel Frost supported the South in the conflict that was just starting to break into open violence. In fact, Frost led a Confederate attack on a government arsenal in St. Louis while the governorship was being discussed. Although Todd was an unequivocal opponent of slavery, and eventually fought on the Union side of the Civil War, his association with Frost was apparently regarded in government circles as an insurmountable obstacle to his appointment as governor. In his place, Lincoln chose another friend from his home town of Springfield, Illinois: Lincoln family physician, Dr. William Jayne. Todd had not lost his influence altogether, however; he seems to have been instrumental in persuading the governor to choose Yankton as his base of operations when he first came to the Territory to organize an interim government in May 1861.[24]

Governor Jayne must have been dismayed by what he saw when, accompanied by Territorial Secretary John Hutchinson, he arrived at Yankton on May 26. No more than a dozen small buildings, several of very primitive construction, interrupted the treeless prairie. These few structures scowled at each other across a weedy, rutted, expanse of mud that was grandly called Broadway on the townsite plan. Both Sioux Falls and Vermillion were larger, faster-growing settlements, and their inhabitants resented the choice of Yankton as the provi-

5. William Jayne

sional capital of the Territory. The designation proved to be a great stimulus to Yankton's development, as Todd and his associates knew it would be.

After conducting a census of the Territory, and establishing an interim court system, Governor Jayne made arrangements for the election that fall of a territorial delegate to Congress, and of members of the Territorial Legislature. Todd won the congressional election handily, and Enos Stutsman was among those elected to the Legislative Council, as the territorial upper house was called.

The election marked a shift in Stutsman's political affiliations. He had always been an outspoken Democrat (of the Douglas anti-slavery variety in recent years). Although he did not yet renounce that affiliation, he was nominated for election by a Republican-Democratic "Union Party" convention, organized to avoid political partisanship during the Civil War emergency. He usually cast his lot with the Republicans thereafter.[25]

Relations between Stutsman and Todd seem also to have changed that summer. Although an 1862 newspaper article indicated that he was still associated with Todd's land company (now known as the Yankton Land and Town Company), the following advertisement, published in June, 1861, makes it clear that Stutsman was engaging in business activities that came very close to competition with his employer:

DAKOTA LAND AGENCY OF ENOS STUTSMAN, YANCTON, (sic), D. T. Prompt attention given to the selection of choice land claims in Southern Dakota; attend to the interest of Settlers and Pre-emptors in the Yancton (sic) Land District; Land Warrants and Scrip bought and sold at current rates; attend to the sale and purchase of claims and Town Lots; and Land Warrants furnished on time to settlers, on reasonable terms. All letters on business, or of enquiry, will be answered by return mail.[26]

Such activities were not necessarily incompatible with his duties as an officer of the Todd company; he probably led many potential purchasers to company land. Nevertheless, he was the owner of considerable property in the area himself,[27] and the temptation must have been great to show a preference for his own land over that of the company. Todd, for his part, began to compete with Stutsman in the field of legal services. He had somehow acquired sufficient legal training to enable him to be called to the Iowa bar in 1858,[28] and he now announced a law partnership with Stutsman's former partner, John Currier, with offices in both Sioux City and Yankton:

J. B. S. TODD,   JOHN CURRIER

TODD & CURRIER

ATTORNEYS AT LAW

WILL practice in the Courts of the Territories of Dakota and Nebraska, and in the State of Iowa – All business entrusted to this firm will receive prompt attention. Offices at
Yancton, (sic) D. T., and Sioux City, Iowa.[29]

Whether these developments were cause or effect of a growing rift between Stutsman and Todd, or whether indeed, there was any rift at that point, is not known. It is clear that they were at odds in later years, however, and it is not unreasonable to speculate that differences began to develop in the summer of 1861.

If 1861 was eventful, 1862 was tumultuous. The excitement began in the early spring with a calamitous flood caused by a huge ice jam on the Missouri below Yankton. Many settlers had to move to high ground, and small boats were able to travel from Yankton to Sioux City across normally dry land, "gliding with ease over fence and field."[30]

Before the waters had receded, a flood of politicians was causing even greater consternation in the tiny community. The first session of the Territorial Legislature, dubbed the "Pony Congress" in recognition of the long horseback journeys required of members representing outlying areas, opened March 17, 1862, in makeshift quarters in Yankton. The diary of a resident describes the appearance of the village on the eve of that occasion:

Yankton contains nineteen buildings, comprising one hotel, two boarding houses, one saloon, one store, two Legislative halls, a Secretary's office, one printing office, one law office, two blacksmith shops, a Surveyor General's and Governor's office, and seven log buildings, six of which are occupied.[31]

During sixty days and nights of roisterous debate – in the Legislature, in the hotel, in the saloon, and in the streets – the invading politicians transformed this sleepy hamlet into a scene of frenetic activity. One of the elected representatives, who reported anonymously to a Sioux City newspaper on a regular basis, described the atmosphere as follows:

...the young capital city of Dakota is, indeed, a "live burg." On every street corner and in every office, shop and hotel in town is heard the busy hum of many voices... Through all the long nights the flickering lamps are seen in the merry ballroom... Wine dinners and wine suppers, wine speeches and wine quarrels, and the hurling of bottles and glasses across tables at the bleeding heads of belligerent councilmen, is one source of occasional amusements exhibited here, with a "free ticket" to spectators.[32]

Violence was common, even on the part of those from whom it would not normally be expected. The same observer, for example, reported a fist-fight at the Ash Hotel between Governor Jayne and a man called Wherry, described as the "late Receiver of the Land Office": "Hair pulling, choking, striking, blood spitting and pugilistic exercises were the order, which were performed with grit and relish."[33] On an earlier occasion the freshly dismissed Speaker of the lower house was thrown through a saloon window by the sergeant-at-arms.[34]

Even legless Enos Stutsman became involved in "physical discussions." Stutsman had an explosive temper, a form of periodic release, perhaps, for the accumulated frustrations of his affliction. As his behavior during the Smutty Bear episode demonstrated, he had no shortage of courage. Although he was no match for a standing adversary, his arms and shoulders were unusually well developed, and if he could get an opponent on the ground, he could be dangerous.[35] One historian tells of a mealtime altercation at the Ash Hotel between Stutsman and a Vermillion councilman. Although not as well documented as the episodes described above, the account is entirely compatible with both Stutsman's personality and the somewhat hysterical atmosphere in which that first session was conducted. It began with a verbal argument:

> ...which erupted in a fusillade of condiment bottles, cups, glasses, and the skeleton of the fowl they were eating. Stutsman was...a noted scrapper with or without his crutches, and he flung himself across the table at his equally enraged fellow attorney. Fortunately, on-lookers separated the combatants before any serious damage was done, and they lived to carry on their conflict in the less dangerous confines of the Council chamber.[36]

The issue that lead to both this incident and those involving the former Speaker was the most controversial of the session: the site of the Territory's permanent capital. The Yankton representatives thought they had assured the confirmation of their town as capital in behind-the-scenes negotiations before the Legislature convened, but the supporters of Vermillion, led by the Speaker of the lower house, launched a strong attack on the arrangement. Tempers flared. The Speaker, when he heard a rumor that the sergeant-at-arms, in league with some of the Yankton supporters, planned to do him violence, appealed to the governor. The governor ordered the posting of an officer and twenty men from the Dakota Cavalry at the legislature. This enraged many members, including Enos Stutsman. A member of the Legislature who was present at the time has described the scene:

> As we enter the room, our attention is attracted to the little chubby, good-looking man on our left, who is making a somewhat stirring speech touching the action of Governor Jayne and Speaker Pinney, in stationing an armed force in the hall of the House of Representatives. This gentleman is the Hon. E. Stutsman of this place, who is called the leading member of the Council.[37]

Following Stutsman's speech, the governor was approached and informed that the Speaker had lied about the likelihood of violence in the legislature. The troops were withdrawn, and the Speaker subsequently resigned. It was at this point that the sergeant-at-arms followed him to Robeare's saloon and threw him through the window. Whether this was a genuinely spontaneous response to the Speaker's accusations, or a belated execution of the sergeant's original intention will never be known. At any rate, the appointment of a less partisan individual as Speaker reduced tensions sufficiently to permit the legislators to agree on Yankton as the permanent capital, with certain other perquisites going to Vermillion and Sioux Falls.[38] A story in a Yankton newspaper a few months later attributes the final selection of Yankton as the capital to "the ability, tact and wise management of Mr. Stutsman."[39]

With the capital question out of the way, the Legislature could finally turn its full attention to the essential task of enacting a body of basic laws for the Territory. Considering the difficulty of the job and the inexperience of the lawmakers, it was performed surprisingly well, and with astonishing speed. By the time the legislative session was two months old, basic civil and criminal codes had been enacted, together with statutes on a great variety of special subjects: the incorporation of local government units, the establishment of ferry-boat services, the creation of a territorial militia, the prohibition of brothels and gaming houses, the fencing of livestock, and many lesser matters. While many of the statutes were borrowed from other jurisdictions, they all had to be scrutinized carefully, and most had to be modified to suit local circumstances. The few legally trained members were called upon to contribute heavily, and Enos Stutsman seems to have been among the most active. One historian credits Stutsman with "performing the principal part of the labor of framing the codes and the general laws passed at this first session."[40]

Not all the legislation concerned public matters. Several private divorce bills were introduced, for example, allegedly at the behest of Stutsman and other lawyer members with clients seeking swift and simple dissolution of their marriages. At the end of April a legislator wrote:

Divorce bills are "all the rage" at present. One of these bills came up in Council last Monday, and was read a first, second and third time and passed in ten minutes. It is believed that the Council is composed entirely of "disunionists"... Some rich letters are read in connection with these divorce bills – in one of which, read today, the wife calls her husband "no better than a wooden man."[41]

6. Dakota Territory Legislature, 1866

Only two of the divorce bills so introduced were finally passed and signed into law by the governor that session, however.

By May 16, when the Legislature adjourned, the members were understandably in a mood to celebrate. Part of the festivities included the convening of a "third house," a parody legislature whose hilarious proceedings continued to delight Dakotans in modern times.[42] For some, Stutsman among them, the celebrations seem to have begun early:

For three nights before the adjournment campfires could be seen in the streets from dark to daylight, around which were seated, wigwam style, electioneering parties of councilmen and representatives, all happily drinking, smoking, eating, singing, snoring, speechmaking and milking cows. I happened to cross the street one morning at the peep of day, and there I beheld beside a smouldering camp-fire, two lusty legislators (Chris Maloney and John McBride) holding a kicking cow by the horns, and a third (John Stanage) pulling his full weight at the cow's tail. On each side of the milkless heifer sat two councilmen (Downer Bramble and Enos Stutsman) flat upon their unfailing foundations, with pails in hand, making sorrowful attempts and vain, at teasing milk enough from the farrow quadruped for their final pitcher of eggnog. Off on one side lay a corpulent representative (Hugh Donaldson) sprawled upon his belly and convulsed with laughter. And there in front of the scene stood another eloquent law-maker (John Boyle) with hat, coat and boots off, making a military speech and appealing to the cow to give down, in behalf of her country.[43]

The energy, ability, and political influence demonstrated by Enos Stutsman were not lost on Governor Jayne. On June 30 he offered Stutsman a two-year appointment as his personal secretary, at a salary of $50 a month.[44] Stutsman's acceptance of the position was both a commitment to the Republican side of the political firmament, and, as it turned out, a further step toward a final rupture of his relations with J.B.S. Todd.

Not long after the occupation of Yankton by territorial legislators had ended, another invasion, infinitely more menacing, loomed. Relations between the Indian and white populations of the northwest, never warm, had deteriorated distressingly during the previous few months. The Indians, on the one hand, were dissatisfied with the terms of their treaties, and disturbed by the continually increasing pressure of white settlement. The whites, for their part, were annoyed by numerous instances of theft and intimidating behavior on the part of some roaming Indians. One of the measures passed by the first session of the Dakota Legislature was a much-resented law prohibiting the presence of Indians off their reservations except with written permission of the Indian agent.[45] A reduction of troops stationed in the northwest caused by the exigencies of the Civil War emboldened some of the more hostile tribes. On August 18 the Santee Indians of Minnesota launched a bloody uprising that resulted in the slaughter of several hundred Minnesota settlers. The repercussions, which extended for thousands of miles, and continued for several years, constitute one of the sorrier chapters of American history. The effect on Yankton was almost immediate and, again, Enos Stutsman was to be found at the center of the action.

When the troops moved against the Santee rebels, they drove them in the direction of the new Dakota settlements. The concern that this news caused among the settlers was heightened by the knowledge that earlier in the month a cavalry patrol had encountered a band of troublesome Santees near Sioux Falls and had ordered them back to their reservation.[46] On August 25, concern turned to dread. Judge J.B. Amidon and his young son were murdered by a group of Indians while working in a hay field less than a mile from Sioux Falls.[47] Three days later the army, fearful of a major bloodbath, ordered the evacuation of all Sioux Falls residents to Yankton. Within the next week the inhabitants of all the other communities in the area also fled to Yankton.[48]

Governor Jayne issued a proclamation on August 30 ordering the establishment of a militia "for home defense," consisting of "every male citizen in the territory between the ages of eighteen and fifty."[49] The residents of Yankton met the following day, elected officers, and set about organizing their defence. Construction of a defensive stockade was commenced immediately. Built of earth and of every available log and plank in the village, the stockade enclosed about a two-block area of Yankton, including the Ash Hotel.[50] Into and immediately around this makeshift bulwark crowded some 300 settlers, short of food, severely cramped for living space, and apprehensive of attack at any moment.

Tension increased when an emissary sent to the reservation of the Yankton Sioux reported that Chief Strike-the-Ree doubted he would be able to prevent his people joining the Santees in the hostilities.[51] Some of the settlers probably began to regret the recent law prohibiting the Indians off the reservation without a pass. Marauding bands appeared at various locations during the first few days of September, and several skirmishes between these bands and the Dakota cavalry on September 6 brought many settlers to the brink of panic.[52] A meeting of married men, held to debate the merits of mass evacuation to Sioux City, was sharply divided. Although the majority decided that it would be safer to stay and fight from the comparative shelter of the stockade than to expose their families to the risk of attack during a retreat to Sioux City, several expressed contrary views, and tempers wore very thin.[53] The morale of the settlers suffered a further blow when the governor and other federally appointed government officers decided to withdraw. Moses Armstrong, whose letters to the *Sioux City Register* constitute a rich lode of information about Yankton's early days, made no attempt to disguise his contempt:

I would scarcely be believed were I to tell you the truth of the conduct, in these trying times, of our weak-kneed, cowardly, runaway officials. To-day there is not one of our officials in the territory... These brave and "loyal" dignitaries, at the first approach of a red man, are the first to leave the country; and with such rapidity do they fly, pale and breathless, for the states that a boy could play marbles on their horizontal coattails. And on they go, governor, secretary, judges, attorney general, clerks, in one wild, panic-stricken express train of "loyal" officials. Well, the people became frightened and looked for Indians and officials, but could see nothing but the vanishing coattails of the latter disappearing on the far shore of the Big Sioux river. Safe in Sioux City, under the protection of four military companies and a battery, these "loyal" officials, like rats in a haystack, stick their heads from under their wives' multitudinous crinolines, and whisper, with white lips, "Are they coming?"[54]

Enos Stutsman did not join the retreat of the bureaucrats. The secretary referred to in the above letter was Territorial Secretary John

Hutchinson. The governor's feisty private secretary elected to stay in Yankton, as he and Joe Presho had in 1859, when they were the only whites among 2,000 restive Sioux. He was prepared to fight for the community he had been instrumental in establishing. He seems, in fact, to have been one of the leaders in the defence of Yankton. He carried the title *colonel* the rest of his life, and it was no facetious reference (as in the case of "Governor" Frank Ziebach of the Third House.)[55] Whether Stutsman was ever officially designated *colonel* is not entirely clear. His name does not appear on the roster of the Yankton company of the militia, and the highest rank mentioned in that list is *captain*.[56] One historian states that the governor appointed Stutsman as paymaster general of the entire militia, with the rank of colonel.[57] Whether or not this is true, there can be no doubt that colleagues who persisted in referring to *Colonel* Enos Stutsman thereafter did so in recognition of the courageous and energetic role he played during the Yankton siege. To his friends, however, he continued to be known by the affectionate abbreviation, "Stuts."

While Stuts may have been officially designated as paymaster, he had no intention of exercising only administrative functions. Several commentators have recorded that he was an excellent marksman,[58] and he was fully prepared to use his skill with weapons in the defence of the settlement. The following account, written some years later by a man who served as a sergeant in the United States Cavalry contingent stationed in the area at the time, leaves no doubt as to the nature and importance of Stutsman's contribution:

There were many acts of heroism performed by the Dakota pioneers while corralled... in the Yankton stockade... Enos Stutsman... was throughout the trying ordeal constantly to be found at the post of danger with his rifle swung across his back and his revolver strapped to his waist, from which... position its muzzle dragged on the earth, and no man was more ready to sacrifice his life, if need be, in the defense of the settlers, women and children, although he had neither kith or kin among them.[59]

Another source credits Stutsman with having been "one of the most active, courageous, and sensible" members of the defending force.[60]

The peak of the crisis was reached the evening of the debate about withdrawing to Sioux City. Lookouts on the hotel roof spotted riders approaching from the east in the fading light. Every available defender took position behind the still incomplete stockade, and waited tensely for the enemy to draw within range. Before any shots were fired however, the settlers realized that the approaching force was not an Indian band at all, but military reinforcements summoned by the local cavalry contingent. As darkness fell, the soldiers rode into the beleaquered settlement to the accompaniment of resounding cheers.[61]

In addition to raising the spirits of the defenders, the arrival of more troops dampened the enthusiasm of the Indians, already cautious due to the determination and apparent effectiveness of the settlement's own defensive measures. This, in turn, facilitated the efforts of Strike-the-Ree, Charles Picotte, and Indian Agent Dr. Walter A. Burleigh, to persuade the Yankton Sioux to remain peaceful. Although the settlers were penned up in the stockade for several more weeks, and they experienced a few new scares (as when a settler's burning of grass near Enos Stutsman's cabin was interpreted by those within the stockade as an Indian attack signal),[62] the threat gradually passed. Isolated incidents of white–Indian hostility persisted in the area for several years, but by late September Stutsman and fellow Dakotans were able to turn their attention to other matters.

Political questions had never been far from the settlers' minds, even during the crisis. Election day for the second session of the Territorial Legislature, and for a new territorial delegate to Congress, had by bad luck fallen on September 1, when the Indian threat was building to a climax. Procedural irregularities were common in frontier elections of that era, but the confused conditions prevailing during the Indian scare led to abuses that were quite astonishing, even by the standards of the time. Governor Jayne had run for the position of congressional delegate against J.B.S. Todd (now *General* Todd as a result of brief service in the Union army). Jayne was at first declared elected, and he actually served in Washington for a while. However, as evidence of irregular and fraudulent voting practices mounted, the result was reversed. Todd went to Washington, and Jayne resumed his medical practice in Illinois.[63] Stutsman handily won re-election to the

Legislative Council, and although he had been a strong Jayne supporter, there is no indication of serious abuses in his own campaign.

Construction of a new legislative building, which had been interrupted by the siege, was resumed as soon as new supplies of lumber arrived, and the work was finished in time for the opening of the second session on December 1. A two-storey frame structure, the building housed the Legislative Council on the upper floor and the House of Representatives below. Although spartan by today's standards, it was a great improvement over the makeshift quarters in which the first legislators had met earlier in the year.

In recognition, no doubt, of both the prowess he had exhibited during the first session and the leadership he had displayed during the recent crisis, Enos Stutsman was chosen by his colleagues as president of the council. He was to hold that position for three successive sessions of the Legislature. With charges and counter-charges of election fraud flying, the early part of the session was even stormier than the spring debate over the capital site. For some counties there were competing delegations of representatives demanding the right to sit, and it took more than two weeks of bitter negotiations before the lower house was able to agree on its membership and get down to work. Stutsman, as presiding officer of the council, seems to have been able to keep clear of most of the controversy, and he began to develop a non-partisan image that stayed with him for most of his subsequent political career. The local newspaper offered this description after he had been chairing council debates for about three weeks:

As a presiding officer he is cool, firm, dignified and liberal. Impartial and usually correct in his decisions, courteous to a fault, he graciously listens to the suggestions of his peers and gratefully adopts those better than his own. Mr. Stutsman is an able legislator, critical, prudent and honest... He is a ready speaker and clear, brief and conclusive reasoner.[64]

While this eulogy was written by a political crony, a consistently similar picture emerges from the comments of other observers. Dakota's leading early historian, who also knew Stutsman personally, states that he "discharged his duties in such an able and impartial manner as to add to the esteem and confidence of his fellow members which he enjoyed in a marked degree."[65] The impartiality may not always have been as real as it seemed; Stutsman was a masterful behind-the-scenes manipulator. The same historian comments:

> He understood that some men in politics were fond of the "loaves and fishes" in the shape of honors; for himself he preferred power and influence, and was willing that others should have the temporary honors, if in return he could be permitted to dictate the policy. He was usually "the power behind the throne."[66]

Part of Stutsman's influence undoubtedly came from his position as private secretary to the governor. He managed to hold on to the position despite Jayne's resignation in April 1863. Before the new governor was finally appointed, in October, there was a lengthy hiatus, during which Territorial Secretary Hutchinson served as acting governor. Stutsman's appointment as private secretary had been for a two-year term: until June 30, 1864. It appears, however, that Stutsman had never written to Jayne formally accepting the offer, a rather unlawyerly oversight. He now attempted to strengthen his legal position by a letter, dated June 30, 1863, accepting the terms of the offer made exactly a year earlier.[67] Whether for this reason or (more likely) because former Governor Jayne recommended it, the new governor, Newton Edmunds, confirmed Stutsman's appointment as his private secretary on the old terms, with the prospect of an increase in salary.[68] Edmunds, a capable, high-minded, rather humorless man, was a Yankton resident, well known to Stutsman. They had both been political supporters of Jayne's.

In accepting the renewed appointment as private secretary to the governor, Stutsman concluded: "Trusting that our personal and official intercourse may be marked by the same cordial understanding, unreserved confidence and mutual esteem, as have heretofore existed in our private walks and political labours."[69] Whether the word *walks* was used in its literal sense (or was merely a synonym for *occupations*, or perhaps even a slip of the pen for *talks*), is not clear. If so, it conveys an interesting image: the tall straight-laced governor strolling along a dusty prairie road, while his jovial, dwarfish secretary hobbles energetically at his side on cut-down crutches, ever attentive and ready with suggestions. As was often the case with Stutsman's political and business associations, the relationship would cool in time, but for the next two years[70] Enos Stutsman continued to be privy to the governor's thoughts.

The break with former colleague J.B.S. Todd was complete by this time. After winning his third consecutive election to the Legislative Council by a large majority in September 1863, an exultant Stutsman placed the following advertisement in the local newspaper:[71]

THANKS

Fellow citizens of the Third Council District – You have again placed me under obligations to you by a second mark of your confidence. Spurning all outside dictation and deaf to the word of slander – in utter disregard of the insane plotting of General J.B.S. Todd, the impotent wrath of General George D. Hill, the shameless bribery of General C.P. Booge, and the priestly edict of their ghostly advisor, you have given me your unwavering and unbought support and reelected me a member of the Territorial Council by the largest vote cast within the District.

Fellow citizens, it is not for the honor nor for the emoluments attached to the position, but it is for your unshaken confidence in my integrity that I now tender my heartfelt thanks. As you never doubted me, I will not insult you by making loud-mouthed promises. My public record, though humble, is well known and I can only offer the past as a guarantee for the future.

Enos Stutsman

The reference to Todd in this announcement concerned his defeat as territorial delegate to Congress by a man of ascending political importance in the Territory: Dr. Walter A. Burleigh. Physician, businessman, bureaucrat and politician, Burleigh had come to Dakota in 1861 as Indian agent for the Yankton reservation. He had been instrumental, together with Strike-the-Ree and Picotte, in preventing the Yankton Sioux joining the Santee rebellion in 1862, and was widely regarded as a capable, personable and generous man. He was also generally believed to have corruptly enriched himself and his family by a variety of blatant misuses of Indian Agency funds. Only his election as delegate enabled him to head off an official investigation of the charges. That does not seem to have damaged his political popularity, however.[72] His influence was greatly enhanced by

7. Walter A. Burleigh

part-ownership and control of the Yankton *Dakotian*, which he acquired just before the 1863 election. Walter Burleigh remained a political force to be reckoned with for some time to come – one of those charming, energetic, unrepentant rogues with which frontier politics was studded. It is not surprising that Enos Stutsman, with his taste for back-room politics, should have cultivated the friendship of Dr. Burleigh. Besides, Burleigh's colorful personality was much more compatible with Stuts's appetite for fun than was that of the dour Newton Edmunds.

The years from 1863 to 1866 were full and fulfilling for Stutsman. Intermingled with public service in the Legislative Council and as superintendent of Yankton County,[73] were more discreet political activities in the governor's office and in Dr. Burleigh's parlor, land speculation, involvement in a ferry business,[74] and a small amount of legal practice. And there were numerous social and leisure activities. He was, for example, one of the principal organizers of the Old Settlers' Historical Association, established in 1863 with a precocious sense of the historic significance of the events experienced by the frontier community during the preceding few years.[75] The following summer he undertook to investigate the extent of a grasshopper plague that threatened the area:

Hon. E. Stutsman is again in town looking as bright and cheering as a silver dollar. He has been for some weeks in Iowa watching the course of the grasshopper army. He says that their ravages fortunately extended but a few miles below Sioux City, and then veered eastward. This will be encouraging news to our citizens, many of whom are already sending out teams to that state to bring in their winter supply of provisions.[76]

He loved travelling, especially to out-of-the-way places:

Hon. E. Stutsman has gone to Crow Creek to remain a few weeks when he will return to his home and friends in Yankton. A favorable opportunity for a pleasant trip to that remote locality presented itself in the steamboat Fanny Ogden, and "Stuts" could not withstand the tempting invitation. We know he will enjoy the ride and lend himself a valuable social acquisition to the circle of passengers.[77]

The motivation for these trips was partly financial – to explore opportunities for land speculation and other commercial ventures in recently opened areas – but he seems also to have derived great personal pleasure from merely seeing new places and meeting new people.

His social talents were often remarked upon by those who knew him:

As his shyness with women testified, there was always a vein of sensitivity lying close to his sunny surface. Outbursts of anger still occurred, though less frequently than they had in earlier years. Local legend tells of an altercation in the hotel dining room between Stutsman and his friend Downer Bramble, that ended in flying crockery and a challenge to duel.[79] According to the story, both protagonists rushed home and strapped on their firearms, but they had regained their composure and common sense before arriving at the field of honor. The story lacks authentication, and is suspiciously similar in some respects to the account of Stutsman's hotel brawl over the choice of Yankton as capital site. Nevertheless, like most legends, whether true or false, it accurately portrays a significant element of its subject's character.

Stutsman was well aware of his impulsiveness, and was sometimes engagingly frank in acknowledging it. In the course of a rather effusive speech accepting his unanimous election as council president for the third time in 1865, he commented:

Fond of good fellowship and friendly intercourse, he is especially gifted in entertaining a social and convivial circle. Subdued and retiring in the society of ladies, yet gallant, urbane and pleasing in wit and humor, "Stuts" is inimitable. He sings a song with much eclat and invariably calls down the House in reading his comical yarns.[78]

There are honorable gentlemen present whose coolness and deliberation in the midst of excitement I have often envied, and vainly sought to imitate. It has pleased the Father of Life to endow me with the quick sympathies of an ardent temperament; and I have very often been painfully conscious of having manifested a warmth of feeling, and, I fear, discourtesy, to honorable gentlemen during your deliberations on measures of more than ordinary interest, which I do as deeply regret as you can possibly condemn. But... the forbearance you have so kindly extended to my faults shall be the good to prompt me to renewed efforts for self-government.[80]

Not everyone would have agreed that his promise of "self-government" was entirely fulfilled that session. A member of the Legislature against whom Stutsman pressed persistent charges of corruption (which historians seem to agree were unfounded), included the following sarcastic passage in his letter of defence:

Of course I do not question the motives of the distinguished mover of that resolution. It cannot be possible that he was actuated by any personal or selfish motives; by any mean desire for petty revenge because of a fancied injury. Oh no! His motives must have been of the highest and most patriotic; he must have had the most ardent desire for the public good.[81]

Stutsman's relations with Governor Edmunds gradually soured. For example, when he applied unsuccessfully for the position of territorial secretary in the spring of 1864, it was to Dr. Jayne rather than to Edmunds that he turned for support.[82] His appointment as private secretary to the governor seems to have ended sometime in 1865; while he appears to have held the position at the beginning of the year,[83] another man held it by autumn.[84] The reasons for his fall from grace are not known, but they probably included both incompatibility of personalities and the secretary's increasing involvement with Dr. Walter Burleigh and his cohorts. For perhaps related reasons, Stutsman failed to be chosen as president of the Legislative Council when the Territorial Legislature assembled for the 1865–66 session.

Freed of the restraints imposed by the secretaryship and the council presidency, Stutsman was able to play a much more free-wheeling role in the 1865–66 session than he ever had before. His mischievous tendencies were more evident. For example, to annoy Governor Edmunds and prolong debate on the governor's message, he introduced a piece of spoof legislation, calling for the encouragement of dogbreeding, the outlawing of puppydrowning, and the establishment of a fund "for the support of superannuated dogs and indigent puppies," which he insisted on discussing whenever the governor's message was being considered by the council.[85]

In 1866, Stutsman collaborated with Walter Burleigh in a scheme to oust Edmunds from the governorship. Incredible as it may seem on the part of a man whose own notorious practices as Indian agent had escaped official investigation only because of his success at the polls, Burleigh accused Edmunds of corruption in the conduct of Indian affairs. Among the documents supporting the charges was a letter, dated April 18, 1866, from Enos Stutsman.[86] The campaign succeeded, and Edmunds was removed in August 1866. His replacement, Andrew J. Faulk, was Walter Burleigh's father-in-law.[87]

By the time the new governor arrived in Yankton to take up his duties, Stutsman had moved on to a more remote part of the Dakota Territory. In February he had accepted an appointment, doubtless offered at the instigation of Congressional Delegate Burleigh, as a special agent of the federal Treasury Department to investigate smuggling and other customs irregularities between the Territory and British North America.[88] By midsummer he had moved to Pembina, on the international boundary, in order to be closer to the scene of the transgressions he was supposed to investigate.[89] A new phase of his career had begun.

CHAPTER THREE

PEMBINA

1866-1869

IN THE MID-1860s PEMBINA WAS BOTH THE OLD-est and the most populous center in the Dakota Territories. But because of its geographic remoteness and the composition of its population, it was the least influential.

Located on the Red River just south of the 49th parallel, and several hundred miles north of Yankton, Pembina had been the site of fur trade posts for more than a century. By the time Stutsman arrived, the area had a settled population of more than a thousand.[1] The form of settlement differed markedly from that of the newly populated districts to the south, however. Most of the inhabitants were Métis. Although they maintained permanent homes in the Red River Valley, the Métis still migrated westward over the plains *en masse* twice annually in pursuit of the rapidly disappearing bison. They were distinct from most of the other residents in dress (featuring colorful headgear, moccasins, and flamboyant sashes), in religion (Roman Catholic), and in language (French). When 200 citizens from the Pembina area petitioned Congress for separate territorial status in 1858, the petition was written in French, and almost all the signatories had French names.[2] Their physical and cultural isolation from the rest of the United States was accentuated by their proximity to British territory, where the population was also predominantly Métis. In fact, in most cases there were extensive family connections straddling the international boundary.

Cultural homogeneity offered one political advantage: the population usually voted *en bloc* at elections.[3] This was seldom sufficient to give Pembina an effective political voice, however. Near the conclusion of the second session of the Territorial Legislature in early 1863, for example, after the Red River members had begun their long journey home, a bill was introduced to wipe out all Red River representation to the Legislature. Pembina voters had supported the Democrats in the 1863 election, and the Republican majority in the Legislature thought that such impertinence deserved to be reprimanded. The bill failed by one vote to receive the necessary two-thirds majority that year,[4] but a similar measure was enacted at the following session. It deprived the Red River Valley of any legislative representation in Yankton for the next three years.[5]

Politicians could not ignore the Red River country much longer. As the economic climate improved and the fear of Indian violence subsided, the demand for new homestead lands grew. Moreover, the westward thrust of railroad steel had made the Red River Valley the principal supply route for the British settlements to the north, and the impending union of British North American colonies held out the prospect of large-scale expansion of those settlements. Both as a transportation corridor and as a potential agricultural settlement, the Red River Valley was beginning to beckon land speculators.

Stepped-up trade across the boundary led to increasing infractions of customs law. Large quantities of British goods, spirited across the unfenced border without the payment of import duties, were showing up in the shops of St. Paul and other American centers. The tiny customs staff stationed at Pembina was unable to cope adequately with this burgeoning problem. As commercial opportunists of all kinds moved into the laxly regulated territory, breaches of other revenue laws, such as failure to pay excise duty on the sale of alcoholic

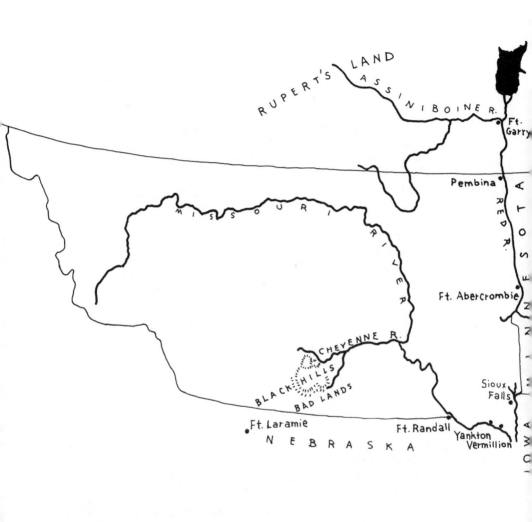

RUPERT'S LAND

ASSINIBOINE R.

Ft. Garry

Pembina

RED R.

MISSOURI RIVER

Ft. Abercrombie

MINNESOTA

CHEYENNE R.

BLACK HILLS

BAD LANDS

Sioux Falls

Ft. Laramie

Ft. Randall

Yankton
Vermillion

NEBRASKA

IOWA

DAKOTA TERRITORY
1861

N.S.

beverages, were also becoming increasingly common. Treasury Department officials in Washington eventually decided to appoint a special agent to investigate and recommend ameliorative measures.

In view of his demonstrated talents, and his cordial relations with territorial patronage dispenser Walter Burleigh, it is not surprising that Enos Stutsman should have been offered the appointment as special agent. Given his taste for adventure, travel, and land speculation, his acceptance was equally to be expected (if, indeed, he had not sought out the position in the first place).

When he first undertook the assignment, in February 1866, Stutsman did not intend to take up residence in Pembina.[6] The territory for which he was responsible was huge (originally Idaho, Dakota and Montana, though soon reduced to Dakota and, eventually, Minnesota[7]), and he thought he could administer it from Yankton. However, his visit[8] to Pembina that summer stretched into a permanent residency. Some writers have suggested that he decided to stay because he fell in love with the Red River country.[9] While it is true that he spoke and wrote enthusiastically about the area, his primary reason for staying in Pembina was more likely the fact that most of his duties involved activities occurring at or near the border. The exhausting nature of travel between Yankton and Pembina no doubt also contributed to his decision.

The first trip north was made in high summer when conditions were at their best; yet Stutsman found the journey tedious in the extreme. It was necessary to take an indirect route: southeast on the Missouri by boat, thence to Clinton, Iowa, on the Mississippi by stagecoach and such incomplete rail lines as existed, north to St. Paul by steamer, westward by stage and rail to Fort Abercrombie on the Red River, and finally down the Red by boat to Pembina.[10] It took 23 days in all. Even a person of Stutsman's stamina and love of travel would not wish to repeat the ordeal often.

Although Stutsman was no doubt delighted to have reached his destination at last, his first impressions of Pembina must have been disheartening. The village was tiny – most of the residents of the area lived outside Pembina – and even by the rough-hewn standards of Yankton it presented a very primitive appearance. A surveyor who

POST OFFICE & RESIDENCE OF CHARLES CAVILEER IN 1860.
PEMBINA, N. DAK.

9. Cavalier residence and post office, Pembina, D.T. 1860

visited the area four years later has left this unpalatable description of the village:

I will never forget my first and only night at old Pembina, its only hotel a log cabin, dirt galore, (where) they served supper of soggy bread, rusty salt pork and Arbuckle coffee... We retired early, found and fought until daylight numerous bedfellows already in possession. When fairly vanquished, I retired from the field of action, dressed, and started for an early appetite-producing walk, when, seeing a number of people on the riverbank interested in something that was going on, I investigated and found, among others, a crowd of... (Indian women), with their youngsters, eagerly watching the cutting-up of a freshly-killed ox, all scrambling and quarrelling for the offal. Returning to the hotel for breakfast, I was served a liberal plate of fresh fried beef, but equally fresh was the scene of a couple of hours before, and I gave the excuse of chronic indigestion for my abstinence, notwithstanding the landlord's assurance that it was fresh-killed that morning. One night was all I wanted in Pembina...[11]

The absence of refined amenities had never troubled Stutsman, however, and he found Pembina generally to his liking. There was, for one thing, more than ample opportunity to indulge his appetite for interesting personalities, and his talent for friendship. Many of those he met in the Ragged Edge Saloon, and The Robber's Nest[12] were classic frontier characters. He would already have known Joseph Rolette, the once-dominant political figure from the area. Joe Rolette was a rough diamond – direct, good-humored, and stubborn. His political reputation was based primarily on his legendary single-handed forestalling of an attempted shift of the capital of the Minnesota Territory from St. Paul to another town in 1857. The bill to bring about the site change appeared to command the support of most legislators. It is said that Rolette, an opponent of change and chairman of one of the committees of the territorial Council, was able to prevent the bill's passage by the simple expedient of disappearing from view, bill in hand, as soon as it was referred to his committee, and staying in hiding until the legislative session was over.[13] Although he was approaching the end of his life when Stutsman arrived in Pembina, his son, Joe Junior, seemed likely to carry on the family tradition.

Other prominent Pembina residents included Charles Cavalier, the lanky, high-spirited merchant and postmaster, with whose family

10. Joseph Rolette

Stutsman took up lodgings on what turned out to be a permanent basis. There was also Joseph Lemay, the collector of customs, who had been attempting for several years to stem the smuggling tide, but had met with indifferent success. Lemay had served the Treasury Department conscientiously, retreating from his post only once during a threat of Indian violence. He was understandably puzzled about Stutsman's appointment, and about the relationship between his duties and those of the mercurial new special agent. He seems to have taken Stutsman's investigative activities and advice in good spirit at the beginning, however.[14] Stuts had doubtless turned on his charm.

Enos Stutsman seems to have carried out his duties as special Treasury agent efficiently and, to a lesser extent, effectively. At the outset he directed a considerable proportion of his efforts to ingratiating himself with his superiors. He learned, for example, that the commissioner of customs in Washington, to whom he was immediately responsible, had an interest in Indian artifacts, and no less than four of his first year's reports enclosed gifts of Indian pipes and tobacco, or information about their manufacture.[15] He should not be judged too harshly for this; the art of "gear greasing" was widely practiced at the time.

His letters also show that he was devoting much thought and effort to the problem of reducing smuggling from the British territories. His first proposals, like those of many other civil servants before and after him, called for increases in staff. A detective was hired, for example, with instructions to remain near the British settlements on the Red River. He was to maintain a vigil on commercial comings and goings, while keeping his purpose "discreet."[16] In making the appointment Stutsman did not follow safe civil service procedures. Perhaps he had been convinced by the failure of an earlier request, through proper channels, for an assistant special agent,[17] that only direct action would produce results. After persuading Collector Lemay to hire the detective immediately,[18] Stutsman handed the man a letter of instruction,[19] and only then wrote to Washington recommending the appointment. He does not seem to have been troubled about the dubious nature of Lemay's authority to hire the detective or about his own authority over Lemay.

11. Charles Cavalier in later life

It must have been very difficult to disguise one's true occupation in small frontier communities, and Stutsman was forced to terminate the detective's appointment after ten months when he learned that the man's identity and purpose had become known to Winnipeg merchants.[20] In the meantime, however, a good deal of useful information had been gathered. It enabled Stutsman to demonstrate, for example, that certain goods allegedly smuggled from Winnipeg to the upper Missouri had probably come from Fort Ellice or Fort Edmonton instead.[21]

Several other persons seem also to have been added to Collector Lemay's staff, often on a part-time basis, during this period. While there is little direct evidence of his involvement in these appointments, the names of such persons as Joe Rolette Jr., and both Mr. & Mrs. Cavalier, on the payroll[22] suggest that Stutsman may have had a good deal to do with them.

The case of Mrs. Cavalier, with whose family Stutsman resided, is particularly interesting. There can be no doubt that Stutsman was instrumental in having her added to the staff. On January 1, 1867, he wrote to the secretary of the Treasury about the need for a female inspector:

Since arriving here, I have discovered that a regular system of smuggling is, and, I am informed, has been carried on through the agency of women. The Stores in the British American Settlement on the Red River are well supplied with fine articles of foreign goods, such as silks, velvets, laces, jewelry, etc., such goods to a very large amount are annually smuggled into the U.S. secreted on the person of women, and afterward disposed of at St. Paul, Minn. This mode of smuggling has been carried on with almost perfect impunity, for the reason of the absence of a suitable Female Inspector of Customs at this Port. It is not to be supposed that male inspectors will make such an examination as would disclose the fact of such concealment...

...I have requested Collector Lemay to nominate a suitable Female Inspector of Customs and... he has nominated to that position, Mrs. Isabella Cavalier... who is well-qualified and in all aspects suitable.[23]

Officials in Washington, concerned about the rising costs of the Pembina office, were not convinced that a female inspector was necessary

12. Isabella Cavalier in later life

and instructed Lemay a few months later to abolish the position after November 1, 1867. But Stutsman was not to be defeated so easily. On October 25 he wrote to Lemay recommending that inasmuch as the services of Mrs. Cavalier were still required, she be appointed as "occasional inspector" on a month-by-month basis, as soon as her regular appointment ended.[24]

The fact that it was thought necessary to record this suggestion in a letter when Stutsman and Lemay were in continuous daily contact indicates that the latter, who was beginning to bridle under Stutsman's asserted authority, questioned the propriety of the proposal. It was only three weeks later that Lemay wrote to the secretary of the Treasury requesting a clarification of Stutsman's position: "Would the Department have the kindness of informing me what the authority of the Special Agent is over me? In this case, for instance the instructions of the Special Agent have left me in doubt as to how I should act."[25] Unfortunately, Lemay did not explain what "this case" concerned. The secretary requested elaboration, but no reply has been preserved. There is at least a strong possibility that Lemay's letter referred to Stutsman's persistent efforts to keep his friend Isabella Cavalier on the customs payroll. In any event, the controversy over the female inspector continued for another year. In March 1868 Stutsman wrote to his immediate superior in Washington renewing his advocacy for a permanent female appointment. He pointed out that men were reluctant to make any inspection of women, and continued:

...And as for looking under a lady's garments to ascertain whether her rotundity is owing to a quantity of said valuable goods, or to some other and more natural cause, is utterly out of the question. But give us a female Inspector, and I warrant you that her woman's curiosity will not allow her to desist short of the *naked* truth.[26]

His arguments seem to have carried the day temporarily, but in September of that year, when the secretary of the Treasury instructed Lemay to eliminate certain positions and to reduce the remuneration for others, Mrs. Cavalier was among the persons dismissed.[27] Whether the episode of the female inspector had been an assiduous attempt by Stutsman to eliminate a genuine abuse, or merely a determined exercise in "porkbarrelling," is not easy to tell. His arguments were certainly persuasive, but the fact that he never referred to a single instance of female smuggling actually detected by Mrs. Cavalier during her year-and-a-half of sporadic employment as female inspector provides reason for skepticism.

If he was prepared to use his position for the advantage of his friends, he was also delighted when the occasion arose to use it for the discomfiture of his enemies. He wrote with evident relish when he reported to his superiors the arrest and prosecution of one of his political opponents, C.F. Rosstenscher, for manufacturing and selling beer in violation of excise laws.[28] Several months previously, in May 1867, he had written to Washington to enquire whether it was: "part of my official duties to investigate and report to the Treasury Department frauds and misapplications of public money by Government Officers – Civil and Military." He suggested that he would have, in that case, "a very wide field for the display of public usefulness."[29] It is not known what reply he received to his request for instructions, but it seems probable that it was negative, since there is no evidence of his having conducted investigations outside the fields of customs and excise. Had he been authorized to swing his investigative axe more sweepingly, there is little doubt that the field would have been strewn with his political enemies.

Many of Stutsman's investigations were conducted personally. In order to form an impression of past and present patterns of smuggling and illicit liquor traffic, he interviewed transportation officials, businessmen, law enforcement officers, and Indian agents from all regions of his vast territory. The Indian agents were particularly informative, because a high percentage of the liquor law violations involved trade with Indians, and Indians were apparently also employed to commit many of the customs violations.

These investigations obliged him to travel great distances under trying conditions. During the month of October 1868 alone, he made two trips to Winnipeg, three to St. Joseph, and several to various border points – 570 miles in total.[30]

He was, true to form, careful to arrange his official travel in a way that would be of greatest advantage to his personal interests. The visits to Winnipeg in October 1868 happened, for example, to occur when he had legal business in that settlement, and his annual journeys to Yankton usually coincided with the sessions of the Territorial Legislature, in which he continued to play a leading role. Interestingly, the letters to the department in which he explained his need to visit Yankton had a somewhat defensive tone, and did not mention the fact that he was an elected member of the Legislature. On October 27, 1868, for example, he began by describing the need for courts in the Red River area, and then continued:

I have therefore concluded while attending to official business on the Missouri River, to visit Yankton during the sitting of our Territorial Legislature in December next, and use my influence with the Members (with all of whom I am personally acquainted) in favor of a redistricting of the Territory into Judicial districts – so as to have the Red River Country created into a Judicial district...[31]

Failure to refer to his own membership in the Legislature cannot be attributed to modesty. However, most of his travel was undeniably integral to his work as special agent, and it is difficult to fault him for being resourceful enough to turn some of it to additional personal advantage.

Steamboat, stage and rail facilities were rudimentary and unreliable, where they existed, and Stutsman was often forced to fall back on much more primitive forms of transport. A published account by an early resident describes in rather glowing terms a journey made with Stutsman on ponies from Pembina to Fort Abercrombie across the uninhabited prairie west of the Red River in the autumn of 1867.[32] It seems romantic until one considers the rough terrain that had to be crossed, the streams that had to be forded, the insects, the fear of Indian depredations, and the fact that one of the riders was legless. It took them a week to travel 140 miles.

Compared to some of his other treks, that journey *was* romantic. The return trip from Yankton the following winter was perhaps his most arduous. Stutsman's description of it in his report to the Treasury Department reveals so much about both Stutsman's personality and the conditions under which he was forced to work that it is worth quoting at length:

Pembina, D.T. Feb. 22nd, 1868.

Sir —

It being my duty to keep you advised of my movements, I have the honor to inform you that after a desperate trip I arrived here on the 17th Inst. – I found more snow between St. Paul and Pembina than usual at this season and it being much drifted I found dog travelling tedious in the extreme.

Owing to the recent formation of the drifts, the crust is not firm – in consequence of which I, now and then, "went under" – It would have amused you to have seen the "Special Agent" and his four dogs scrambling to view in a promiscuous and demoralized condition. But while it would have seemed capital fun when viewed by a disinterested party, *I* could not see it. Ordinarily I use only 3 dogs, but I added a fourth and found I had none too many. – My first, second and third dogs are white, but as persons travelling in this latitude in winter are liable to snow-blind (sic) unless there be some dark object to rest the eye upon, I purchased one black dog. Furthermore, as our late Legislature struck the word "white" from the School and Election laws, I deemed it my duty as well as quite proper to have at least *one* black or "Colored" dog in my train. But not wishing to appear quite *too* "radical" I put said "Colored" dog behind and propose keeping him there until his good conduct and education warrant promotion. Or, at least, until I know the complexion of the next Administration.

If some of our *fat* Dakota Officials, sitting in their well-furnished Offices, warmed by Uncle Sam's wood, and sipping their hot brandy bought with said indulgent Uncle's money, were called to make such a Laplandish journey, O, would they not send up such a wailing and lamentation as would drown the groans of the very damned!

For a few days I traveled in company with the mail train, the Half Breed driver of which is one of the most brutal and inhuman things I ever saw. His cruel treatment of his unoffending dogs so disgusted and sickened me that I ordered my driver to part company with him.

Had I but the ordering of things for a brief time, I would condemn such monsters to a limited confinement in the very coldest nook of the Spirit Land where the mercury never rises about 40° below zero – and there to stand as a _____ post for the very meanest dogs in purgatory.

After I have visited the several stations along the International line, I will prepare and forward my annual report.[33]

That he struck off on his own in such dangerous conditions because of unhappiness with the mail-train driver's treatment of his dogs says a good deal about Stutsman's independence and courage. That he could look back on the whole experience with such salty good humor testifies to his roguish charm.

It did not take Stutsman long to realize that only a small fraction of customs and excise infractions could possibly be brought to light with the minimal law enforcement machinery then in place in the area. In May 1867 he reported the seriousness of the problem to Washington, and pleaded for the early establishment of a military garrison at Pembina:

Since reaching the Missouri River I have ascertained the fact that during the past year, and particularly last winter, smuggled goods in large quantities have been introduced into the Indian Country at and in the vicinity of Devils Lake by traders residing in British America, and disposed of to the several bands of hostile and semi-hostile Sioux.

These goods (Arms, Ammunition, Blankets, Cloth, Alcohol, Trinkets, Notions, etc.) were crossed at points from fifty to seventy-five miles west of Pembina, so remote from white settlements and in the heart of the Indian Country, that the chance of taking them in the act or after being introduced would stand about one in fifty. – And after reaching a point within striking distance of Devils Lake it would have been sheer madness to attempt their seizure, for the reason that the hostile Indians regard the smugglers as their friends, and will at all times make common cause with them against officers of the Government.

With this extensive traffic carried on under our very nose, we can only stand off in utter helplessness and derive whatsoever consolation we can from the reflection that it is not within *our* power to prevent or punish the offense.

And this condition of things must exist until such time as the U.S. Government shall determine to compel a due respect for its laws, which can only be done by a suitable disposition of military force near the British line.

Should the proposed military post to be erected on the Scheyenne (sic) River be located sufficiently near the infested district to afford protection to the Revenue Officers, it will go far toward preventing the contraband traffic. But what, most of all, is needed – is the establishment of a military post at Pembina – an appropriation for which has, I am informed, been made – but upon which the War Department have thus far taken no action. With a military post at Pembina, and one on the Scheyenne I will undertake to promise that sm ¬ling, in any large amounts, on our northern line will be forever at an end.[34]

During the remainder of his term as special agent, Stutsman missed few opportunities to remind the department of the futility of attempting to prevent smuggling across a thousand-mile wilderness frontier without adequate military or judicial support.[35] His assiduousness in this regard was no doubt augmented by his awareness that the security afforded by the presence of a military garrison would encourage immigration, and thereby enhance the opportunities for land speculation.

The government did not seem to share his sense of urgency about these matters. Although both military and judicial assistance were eventually provided, it was not forthcoming during Stutsman's tenure as special agent. In fact, in September 1868 the Department ordered Lemay to dismiss certain members of his staff (including Mrs. Cavalier) and to reduce the compensation paid to others. Stutsman's protest was indignant.[36] He began by pointing out that the order had been recommended by another special agent:

...who it seems came no further West than St. Paul – 500 miles from this frontier post, and could not have based his opinion upon a personal knowledge of the country – and I am quite sure that until he visits this locality in person, he will not have a correct idea of the extent of the frontier to be *garded* (sic), and the labor required to transact the business, owing to the fact that several thousand single ox or horse carts are employed in transporting imports, exports, and travel.

He explained that there was a big difference between Pembina and typical ports of entry on oceans or lakes. Whereas goods carried by ship could by inspected in bulk, prairie transportation was by individual carts travelling in small brigades (over 4,000 carts the previous year) which required much more detailed attention. A larger staff was therefore necessary to inspect a given quantity of merchandise than in the case of an ocean port. He concluded by arguing that the economy measure would end up costing the government money:

During the last fiscal year the duties and fees received here amount to $19,448.78, while the salary and per diem paid the Collector, Deputies, and Inspectors amount to $10,527.50 – which after deducting $1,895.46 expended at St. Paul for the relief of the unusually large number (66) of hospital patients, shows a clear profit to the Government of $7,025.82. And let it be remembered that this is the result at a North Western frontier post, on the very verge of civilization, and utterly destitute of protection or aid from the Military or the Courts.

. . .

Reduce the number of competent Inspectors – the frontier cannot be properly *garded*, (sic) and heavy smuggling will be the natural *consequence*.

Reduce the compensation – the present high price of provisions will render it impossible to secure the services of reliable men – and the Collector will be compelled to take into the public service unsuitable men who by a single blunder, neglect or connivance may subject the government to a loss of several thousand dollars.

By dropping one Inspector and the Female Inspector, and taking 50 cents per day each from the compensation of three Inspectors, you will save an expenditure of $2,007.50. But I fear you will also reduce the collections twice that amount.

Although hampered by inadequate staff and minimal law enforcement facilities, Stutsman was successful in uncovering a number of major revenue offenses. One of the most serious of his discoveries related to large-scale smuggling by Winnipeg merchants in earlier years – 1863 and 1864. After he reported these offenses in October 1868, the department ordered that the persons accused be prosecuted, and then dismissed Joseph Lemay, under whose tenure as customs collector the smuggling had occurred.[37]

Whether the dismissal was prompted by Stutsman's report is not clear. A Winnipeg newspaper suggested that Lemay was let go for political reasons, there being a new administration in Washington.[38] On the other hand, Lemay had been reprimanded for errors in the past, including a recent controversy over breach of a certain transportation bond,[39] and a letter informing him of Stutsman's report, peremptory in tone, came shortly before his suspension.[40] Even if the report was not the cause of his being fired, Lemay no doubt thought it was; there was open hostility between Lemay and Stutsman from that point on. The rift may have had serious consequences for the history of the northwest.

The Treasury Department instructed Lemay's successor to have Stutsman arrange prosecution of the merchants named in his report as smugglers. How he could have accomplished this in a jurisdiction that did not yet have any courts, and in circumstances where most or all of the defendants were in another country, was not explained. In any event, Stutsman himself was relieved of his duties as special agent not long afterward,[41] and the matter does not appear to have been pursued further.

Stutsman's dismissal was no reflection on his performance as special agent. Like his appointment to the position in the first place, it was entirely a matter of political patronage. It constituted, in fact, the first serious sign of mortality in his hitherto charmed political life. The skill with which he attempted to avoid dismissal, or at least to preserve a relatively healthy political position afterward made it clear that his political career was far from finished, however.

The political scene that prevailed during Stutsman's three years as special agent was kaleidoscopic. The years after Lincoln's death had been turbulent, especially at the national level. Andrew Johnson, catapulted from the vice presidency to a complete term as chief executive, soon lost the confidence of Congress as a result of his policy of moderation in the reconstruction of the southern states, and his immoderate criticism of the more extreme policies espoused by the ascendant radical wing of the Republican Party. Any doubt on this score was removed by the 1866 congressional election, in which radical majorities were returned to both House and Senate. Although he survived the impeachment proceedings of early 1868, Johnson retained no political capital, and the Republican convention chose General U.S. Grant, the darling of the radicals, to contest the presidential election that fall.

Stutsman, it will be remembered, though originally a Democrat, had hitched his wagon to the political star of Dr. Walter Burleigh, the Republican territorial delegate to Congress. Burleigh was a staunch supporter of Andrew Johnson and his moderate reconstruction policies. Although his personal popularity and his adroitness in marshalling the endorsements of both Democrats and moderate Republicans enabled him to breast the anti-Johnson tide in the 1866 congressional election, the ever-increasing strength of the Grant forces cast doubt on Burleigh's political future as the 1868 election approached. Enos Stutsman's political life, governed by the same factors, was subject to similar uncertainty.

Up to that point, Stutsman's political endeavors had continued to be marked by great success. Having previously assured Burleigh by letter that he thought Burleigh's father-in-law, Andrew Faulk, would make a fine Governor,[42] he wrote an obsequious letter to the new governor immediately after his inauguration in 1866, congratulating him on the appointment, and declaring his allegiance to the administration and policies of President Johnson.[43] The support of Governor Faulk and the Washington administration was to stand him in good stead over the next couple of years.

In the same letter, Stutsman gloated at the thought of his former employer, Newton Edmunds, being stripped of authority:

O, would it not have done my soul good to have been at Yankton when you arrived there, and relieved "His Excellency"? of his honors and responsibilities. Poor, Poor Newton! how his heart must pine for the sweet moments of honor and power – to say nothing about the worshipped dollar. For a long time past he has been stabbing the Dr. (Burleigh) in the back, and now retribution has at last come upon him – and O, how justly. That man Edmunds would sell Christ, as well as his last friend for *less* than "thirty pieces." And he has fallen, as every man must *first* or *last* do, who will betray his friend.[44]

It would be interesting to know whether Stutsman, who had once been an ally of Edmunds, and who occasionally demonstrated a capacity for self-knowledge, recognized the irony in these words.

For the first year he was based in Pembina, he did not hold political office himself. The Red River country continued to be deprived of representation in the Territorial Legislature in accordance with the disenfranchisement law passed in 1864.[45] It was therefore necessary for Stutsman, once he made the decision to reside in Pembina, to submit his resignation as a member of the Territorial Council.[46] He remained politically active nonetheless. Immediately after the 1866 congressional election he mailed the voting returns for the district to the Governor – indicating 103 votes for the governor's son-in-law, Burleigh, and not one for the opposition![47] He had clearly learned quickly how to play the bloc-voting game favored in the Métis districts. It is also interesting to note that the envelope containing the returns was sent unsealed to the governor for perusal. Stutsman's letter of enclosure concludes as follows: "After examining the returns you can seal up the envelope and deliver same to...(the Territorial Secretary) to be laid before the board of Territorial Canvassors."

Although not present in Yankton during the 1866-67 session of the Legislature, Stutsman seems to have accomplished a very important legislative reform at long distance. The Legislature finally re-enfranchised the Red River Valley that session, by passing a law creating and organizing Pembina County.[48] Stutsman claimed to have been responsible. In the letter, March 1867, in which he first announced to the Treasury Department that his "official services" were required in the Missouri River country for a while, he stated: "By representing the pressing necessity for the same, I succeeded in procuring from our late legislature a county organization for the Red River portion of Dakota, which will greatly aid the custom officers here in the efficient performance of their duties."[49] Given his previous influence with the Legislature and his excellent relations with Faulk and Burleigh, this claim rings true.

His assertion that the political organization of the Red River Valley and its representation in Yankton would contribute to improved enforcement of revenue laws was no doubt also true, but this was not likely his chief motivation. For Stutsman the major significance of the new status for the Red River country was the opportunity it provided to re-establish the political base he had been forced to relinquish when he moved to Pembina. He wasted no time availing himself of the opportunity.

In October, 1867, Enos Stutsman was elected by acclamation as the Pembina County representative to the Territorial House of Representatives.[50] Arriving in Yankton in late November (after an exhausting journey that began, as mentioned earlier, with a week's journey on horseback over the forbidding prairie) he discovered that his personal influence had not diminished. When the Legislature opened he was chosen as Speaker of the House by a vote of 12 to 10 over the official Republican Party nominee. The Yankton newspaper attributed this somewhat surprising triumph to Stutsman's personal popularity:

The election of Mr. Stutsman as Speaker of the House, over the Hon. John L. Jolley, was undoubtedly owing to the great personal popularity of the former gentleman. The fact of his being one of the oldest residents of the Territory, with five years of Legislative experience during which time he has ranked high as a parliamentarian and debator, together with his social and genial nature, made him a competitor for the Speakership almost invincible.

We are satisfied that no other man from the Red River country could have been elected, and we believe no other man nominated in opposition to Col. Jolley, the straight republican nominee, could have defeated that gentleman. – The withdrawal of Col. Moody from the contest and the selection of Mr. Jolley, by the Republican caucus, as their standard bearer, just upon the eve of the organization, did not give the latter gentleman time to organize his friends for the contest. Some of those upon whom he relied, and whose votes he would have received had he known sooner that he was to be the Republican candidate, were pledged to his opponent before he reached the Capital. As it was, Col. Jolley received the straight vote of his party, and came within three votes of an election.[51]

The same article pointed out that although he had defeated the Republican Party candidate, Stutsman's election should not be seen as a victory for the Democratic Party, because he "has acted with the Republicans of the country since the commencement of the late war."[52] Although he counted, as did Johnson, Burleigh and the other moderate Republicans, on support from Democratic quarters, Stutsman was never again to admit to a Democratic affiliation. A year later, in fact, he was to refer contemptuously to the official Democratic party newspaper: "For a week or two past our mail sacks have come to us stuffed with 'Dakota Democrats.' They answer pretty well for bum fodder – 'This and nothing more.'"[53] He was committed to the Republican cause, and if things got too hot in the moderate camp, a safer escape route lay in the direction of the radical Republicans rather than back to the Democrats.

Stutsman's acceptance speech upon election as Speaker of the House, was brief:

Gentlemen of the House of Representatives:

In selecting me to preside over your deliberations, you have conferred upon me an honor, as unmerited as it has been unsolicited and I accept the responsible trust with many misgivings, feeling as I do, that there are gentlemen on this floor who possess a fitness for the position which I can only strive to emulate. But as you have seen fit to place me in the chair, I will endeavor to discharge the duties thereby imposed to the very best of my ability, and as patiently and impartially as it is possible for one of my impulsive temperament; this I can promise, and nothing more.[54]

His assertion that the position was unsolicited can, in light of the newspaper's remarks about uncommitted members being buttonholed before Stutsman's opponent arrived in town, be put down to empty rhetoric. His acknowledgement of having an impulsive temperament was certainly accurate, though. He seems to have made a conscious and generally successful effort as Speaker to hold his temperament in rein, and to fulfill the promise of able, patient and impartial chairmanship.[55]

An example of the dispatch and diplomacy with which Stutsman performed the duties of Speaker occurred during that first session, in early January, 1868. On January 6 Governor Faulk wrote to him, as Speaker, exercising his veto over a bill relating to civil procedure in the territorial courts.[56] In the governor's view the bill was incompatible with certain provisions in the Organic Act of the Territory. Although he was not a lawyer himself, Faulk had received representations to this effect, as well as other complaints about the bill, from certain members of the territorial bar and bench. Stutsman replied the same day with a carefully written refutation.[57] In addition to his own cogent arguments, he mentioned that he had taken the trouble to discuss the matter with the chief justice. The views of the chief justice had, he said, been misrepresented, and were in fact favorable to the bill except for a small item that would be amended. Faced with this prompt and persuasive response, the governor relented. He signed the legislation the following day.[58]

Stutsman was much more actively involved in the debates and in the formulation of legislation that session than is customary for Speakers. He left the chair to engage in debate from time to time, and he introduced no less than five bills. The bills were all memorials addressed to Congress, requesting various improvements for the Red River country: a public survey, a military post at Pembina, a land office for the Valley, a mail route to St. Joseph, and a road from Fort Abercrombie to Pembina (the route he had traversed on horseback on his way to attend the assembly that fall).[59]

In support of his efforts to direct the attention of government and others to the Red River Valley, he prepared a report in January 1868 for the Joint House–Council Committee on the Agricultural and Mineral Resources of Dakota Territory, describing the physical features, climate, and economic prospects of the region.[60] It was an attractive account, rendered even more so by the writer's avoidance of exaggerated claims. Considering that Stutsman had resided in the area for only about eighteen months, the range of information presented in the report was impressive. He had obviously made good use of his extensive travel as treasury department agent. Generally speaking, the description was accurate. He must have had occasion, however, as he struggled through gigantic snow drifts on the previously described journey back to Pembina a month later, to repent of the following passage:

The great dread of deep snow, and cold winters in so high a northern latitude is altogether imaginary. The average depth of snow for the last ten years has not exceeded sixteen inches... and while the murcury (sic) may fall to even thirty-five degrees below zero, owing to the absence of high winds the weather does not seem rigorous, nor does it seem as cold as it does in Michigan or Ohio, when the murcury is at, or even from five to ten degrees above zero.

The snow does not drift as in open prairie countries, and as good sleighing can be relied upon, no trouble is experienced in winter travelling.

On the other hand, as he picked himself up from his overturned dog sled for the twentieth time, or huddled in a snow-covered tent waiting for blizzards to abate, he may have found comfort, if not warmth, in recalling the words with which the *Union and Dakotian* had described the conclusion of the legislative session:

Hon. Enos Stutsman presided on this occasion with the same dignity and urbanity which uniformly characterizes his discharge of all like duties, and we were glad to witness that among all those over whom he has presided for the last forty days not one but awarded him the credit of having been decorous and impartial at all times, and zealous in promoting all measures which looked to the general good.[61]

When election time arrived again, in October 1868, the local and national political cauldrons had both reached rolling boils. Stutsman was by then aware that the factions with which he was associated had fallen out of favor. Although he had tried to downplay formal party affiliation in the past in order to attract a multipartisan personal following, he had been widely identified with Walter Burleigh and the moderate Republicans for quite some time. After the Republican Party had rejected the Johnson moderates and had opted for Ulysses S. Grant, the immensely popular "radical," as its presidential candidate, the association with Burleigh became increasingly uncomfortable. Grant seemed assured of an easy victory, and Stutsman, as a Johnson appointee, knew that his appointment as special treasury agent was in jeopardy. At first he seemed content merely to dissociate himself from the Democrats, and to hope that Burleigh's favored candidate for congressional delegate would be elected, and would continue to control patronage under the new administration.[62] However, two events occurred just before the election which caused him to take a dramatic change of direction.

Until then there had been only three candidates for the position of congressional delegate. The Republicans, now controlled by Grant radicals even in the Territory, had nominated Territorial Secretary S.L. Spink. Incumbent delegate Walter Burleigh had then organized a People's Party convention, which chose a well-known judge, J.P. Kidder. Whether Burleigh had hoped for the People's Party nomination himself is not clear, but he seems to have thrown his initial support behind Kidder. The Democrats, running as a separate party for the first time in the Territory, had selected Stutsman's one-time employer, General Todd. Although Todd was a largely spent political force by then, he would likely assist Spink by attracting Democratic votes away from Kidder.

Until some time in early October, Stutsman intended to support Kidder. He wrote to Governor Faulk to that effect on September 28. Although he chided Faulk for permitting the Democrats to split away and create a "triangle fight," and acknowledged the possibility of a Spink victory, he stated unequivocally that the Red River Valley would be voting for Kidder: "Our vote this fall will be small, but so far as I have heard, every vote will be cast for Judge Kidder. – We have only *one* ticket – 'Old Kidder'."[63]

Shortly after writing that letter, however, Stutsman heard news that caused him to shift his allegiance. A large population of railroad workers and miners had sprung up in the vicinity of Laramie and other settlements in Wyoming. Although part of the Dakota Territory, these settlements were some 800 miles away from Yankton, and had very little in common with the rest of the Territory. They had been granted separate territorial status the previous year, but President Johnson had not yet got around to implementing the legislation. They would therefore be entitled to vote for the Dakota delegate to Congress. Walter Burleigh had travelled to Laramie in September, ostensibly to raise support for Judge Kidder. Little support was forthcoming, however, and Burleigh suddenly announced while he was in Wyoming that *he* would be a candidate for re-election. Judge Kidder's backers were furious, and everyone else was confused. The confusion multiplied when a fifth candidate was nominated, a week before election day, by a group of Wyoming residents.

In a somewhat distraught letter to Faulk on October 9, Stutsman announced that "had this information arrived here a little sooner," he and the Red River voters might have "rolled in a full vote for Spink to assist... against the unjust interferences of Wyoming," but that "we shall probably let the vote on Delegate go by default."[64] He quickly shook off this defeatist attitude, however, and began to organize Red River support for radical Republican Spink. Although he may have been sincere in saying at the outset that he did this to meet the Wyoming threat, he soon began to realize that the Burleigh maneuver had presented him with a heaven-sent opportunity to abandon the sinking ship of the moderate Republicans and to sign on with the Grant crew.

Spink won the election by a substantial margin, a result that Stutsman could have predicted almost as easily as he could have forecast Grant's resounding presidential victory. In Pembina County there were 43 votes for Spink and only 12 for Kidder.[65] Immediately after the election, and before the complete results were known (though they could be guessed) Stutsman wrote a remarkable letter to his superior in the Treasury Department. It was obviously designed to distance him as much as possible from the outgoing administration:

Private

Pembina, D.T.
October 15,1868.

Hon. A. Sargent,
Comm. of Customs

Sir —

In the midst of your official duties I am sorry to bother you with matters of a political nature personal to myself – but in as much as it appears from the public Journals that the Hon. Secretary of the Treasury does not favor the election of General Grant, I deem it my duty as one of the employees of the Treasury Dept. to advise him through you of my course in the contest for Delegate in this Territory, which was determined by our Election on the 13th Inst. –

Mr. S.L. Spink (our Territorial Secry.) was nominated for Delegate by the Grant Party; Hon. J.P. Kidder (one of our Associate Justices) was nominated for said office by the Peoples Party; General J.B.S. Todd was nominated by the Democratic party. And in as much as Wyoming remains a portion of Dakota until her federal officers are appointed, confirmed, and qualified (according to a provision of this Organic Act) it seems that the people of that, soon to be, Territory have cast their vote for one of their *own* Citizens as Delegate from *Dakota*.

Personally, I should prefer Judge Kidder to either of the gentlemen named – but regarding his chances, as well as those of Genl. Todd, quite hopeless, as against the Wyoming vote. As a Dakotian, I deemed it but just and proper that the people of Dakota should unite upon their strongest man in order to prevent a Wyoming man to be elected over their heads as *their* Delegate in Congress. I therefore cast my vote, and induced 5/7 of the voters of this county to go for Mr. Spink. –

My course, as above stated, will probably give offence to Dr. Burleigh (our present Delegate), Gov. Faulk, Judge Kidder, Genl. Todd, as well as a majority of the federal Officials of the Treasury, all of which however I am able to stand. But should the Hon. Secretary of the Treasury or yourself not approve of my action in the premises, I do not expect to retain my position of Special Agent. And if the Hon. Secretary or yourself *disapprove* – will you not have the goodness to advise me of the same, so that I may have the *pleasure* of resigning, without waiting until my offical head is cut off like a devoted gobbler at Thanksgiving?

Humbly craving your pardon for thus bothering you –

I beg ever to remain

Yours truly

Enos Stutsman,
(as yet) Special Agent.[66]

Although he was not dismissed as special agent by the outgoing administration, as he had apparently hoped, Stutsman's last-minute change of direction seems to have succeeded in insulating him from the moderate Republicans, and aligning him with the victorious Grant forces. The Republican newspaper, *Union and Dakotian*, reporting the results on October 31, proclaimed his allegiance to the new administration:

The fact is, Red River has surpassed our most sanguine expectations. We had not counted on a majority, but with such energy and popularity as our old friend and townsman, Hon. Enos Stutsman brought to bear against the opposition there, the foe fell back, routed and ruined. "Stuts" stood true to Grant... and Spink, notwithstanding that he was beseiged by bushels of most endearing epistles and many promises... [67]
One wonders whether, when he read the statement that he had "stood

true to Grant," Stutsman remembered having written, in a letter to Governor Faulk only two years previously, that he would "stand true" to the moderate reconstruction policies opposed by Grant and the "mad politicians" in Congress:

I am afraid that the popular mind has not yet cooled sufficient for sound judgment. But Mr. Johnson's policy is clearly right, and being right, *must* ultimately be adopted by the people, if the Union, indeed, is ever to be reestablished in spirit as well as in name. These, from the commencement, having been my convictions, I have and will stand true to the Administration men in their struggle with mad politicians.[68]

Knowing that this change of political affiliation had put his friendship with Dr. Walter Burleigh at risk, Stutsman attempted a reconciliation in March 1869. He wrote to Burleigh congratulating him on speeches he had made in Congress just before his term as territorial delegate expired. Remarking that "(s)ince you are no longer in office, you cannot believe that my commendation is intended to flatter or curry official favor," he claimed to be: "... proud of you as a 'Dakotaian.' – Under your erratic exterior are hid sterling abilities, and with all your faults 'I love you still'."[69] Whether the letter had the desired effect of resuscitating the Stutsman – Burleigh friendship is not known. Burleigh was himself so thoroughly versed in political chicanery that he might well have accepted Stutsman's new allegiance with a cynical chuckle. However, Stutsman subsequently took part, as an influential member of the Grant Republicans in the Territorial Legislature, in a petition to Washington to remove Governor Faulk, Burleigh's father-in-law and Stutsman's former patron, from office.[70] That may well have been too much for Burleigh to forgive and forget.

Despite the shrewdness of his defection to the Grant camp, Stutsman was unable to retain his position as Treasury Department special agent. What he had not counted on was a change in patronage patterns. Whereas in the past most of the federal government patronage in the Territory had been distributed by the congressional delegate, control shifted under the Grant administration to the new governor, John A. Burbank. Burbank tended to favor "carpetbag" appointees from outside the region, and by midsummer, 1869, a new, non-resident, special Treasury agent had been appointed for the area.

At the territorial level, Stutsman fared better. He was easily re-elected to the Territorial House for the 1868–69 session, and although not chosen as Speaker again, he continued to play a central role. Being relieved of the Speakership left him freer than before to participate in the legislative activities of the House, and he threw himself into the work with characteristic verve. He was made a member of four regular House committees: judiciary, railroads, elections, and enrolment. As well he was chairman of a special committee on House rules.[71] His chief concern continued to be for the welfare of the Red River district, and he succeeded in procuring the passage of another memorial seeking a United States land office for the area, and a bill authorizing the establishment of ferries on the Red River. He also took great interest in questions of broader concern, one of the most important of which was female suffrage. Stutsman's sponsorship of votes for women was one of the earliest attempts in the United States to bring about this highly controversial electoral reform.

The *Union and Dakotian* for December 19, 1868, announced the launching of the crusade for female suffrage:

(T)he most radical measure yet introduced in the House is the bill conferring the right of suffrage on women. A gallant representative from Pembina, Hon. Enos Stutsman, has the distinguished honor of being the author of the bill.[72]

A week later the same newspaper commented:

(W)hether it will pass... cannot yet be determined; the chances, however, seem to be about equally balanced. Should the bill pass and become a law Dakota will at once attain notoriety. It will be a sort of mecca, a political haven toward which all the strong-minded like... Susan B. Anthony... and those of the "revolution" stripe will immediately direct their steps.[73]

Alas, the attempted revolution failed. It had attracted widespread attention in other jurisdictions however,[74] and, as the newspaper had predicted, the vote was close. The House had first referred the bill to the Committee on Elections, which Stutsman chaired. That committee, while approving the measure, recommended that the House discuss it fully in Committee of the Whole before proceeding futher. The tone of the committee's report, which Stutsman wrote, clearly supported the legislation, however: "While your committee favor the bill, they believe that a measure so far in advance of old fogy notions should be submitted to general discussion and careful consideration."[75] He was able to steer the bill safely through the House discussion and debate; it passed by a margin of 14 to 9.

In the council the opposition was much stiffer. The leader of the attack on the bill in that chamber (who, by the way, was the brewer, C.F. Rosstenscher, against whom Stutsman had just launched the prosecution for excise abuse) first attempted to delay the matter by introducing a resolution inviting women to come to the council and express their views. He hoped, no doubt, that the session would be over before arrangements could be completed to hear the ladies or, better still, that reticence on the part of most territorial women to engage in public speech-making would create an impression of lack of interest in the question. When this ploy failed to obtain majority support, Rosstenscher moved a substitute bill to replace that which the House had passed. Although its exact contents are not known, the substitute bill seems to have been a facetious affair (one writer used the term *burlesque*[76]), which those who genuinely advocated female suffrage could not accept. When the council passed the substitute bill by an eight to five majority, and the House refused to approve it, Stutsman's noble reform died aborning.[77] Whether it had been the product of genuine conviction, of high spirits, or of a belief that the first politicians to support votes for women would be the principal beneficiaries when the reform was eventually passed, is a matter for speculation.

Losing the appointment as special treasury agent does not seem to have hit Stutsman too hard. He was by this time in a fairly favorable financial position, and he was contemplating a return to law practice, and to more active land speculation. At the point in the 1868 congressional delegate election when he expected Spink to win, but had not yet decided to withdraw his support from Kidder, he hinted in a letter to Faulk that he was reconciled to the loss of his federal appointment:

In the great squabble for office and place, you Slope men need not count me in. I have tried Office, and find it does not pay, and, as a mere experiment, I intend to retire to private life and see if I can not make an honest living! I shall probably spend much of my time on the British side of the line... [78]

North of the border was the town of Winnipeg (still sometimes known as Fort Garry or Red River), which Stutsman had occasionally visited in connection with his customs duties. It was a considerably larger and somewhat more advanced community than Pembina, and Stutsman could see that it had attractive long-range commercial prospects. The immediate cause for his enthusiasm, however, was the possibility of setting up a substantial law practice in the British settlement. His letter to Faulk reported on his successful defense, a few days previously, of a young man charged with manslaughter in the British courts. He obviously expected this victory to bring in more legal business. The name of the case was *The Queen* v. *Alexander McLean*. The Winnipeg *Nor'Wester* called it a *cause célèbre*. [79]

CHAPTER FOUR

THE McLEAN TRIAL

SEPTEMBER 1868

THE McLEAN FAMILY FARMED AT PORTAGE la Prairie, on the Assiniboine River, fifty miles west of Winnipeg. The settlement derived its name from the fact that it was the terminus of a long portage between Lake Manitoba and the Assiniboine River – a portage that linked the eastern and western sections of the fur trade's transcontinental canoe route between Montreal and the Rocky Mountains.

The community suffered from a total absence of governmental or law enforcement facilities. Although the vast territory above the 49th parallel between the Great Lakes and the Rockies was a possession of Great Britain, it lacked the normal British colonial administration. Instead, it was subject to an unusual and increasingly inappropriate form of commercial government.[1] In 1670 the British Crown had granted a charter to the Hudson's Bay Company, bestowing both ownership and governmental responsibilities for the area on the company. While the country remained no more than the site of transient fur-trading operations, this arrangement worked reasonably well, but rudimentary company justice became less and less satisfactory as non-fur-trade settlement increased.

When the first colony of British immigrants was established by Lord Selkirk on the future site of Winnipeg in 1812, the company created a special political structure for the settlement and the area immediately around it. This special enclave was called Assiniboia. By 1868 the legal and governmental machinery of Assiniboia had evolved considerably, although it was still seriously inadequate.

The residents of Portage la Prairie were in a worse position. Because their settlement lay outside the boundaries of Assiniboia, they did not have the benefit of even the simple legal machinery available to those who lived in Winnipeg and vicinity. An attempt early in 1868 to form an indigenous government (called the Republic of Manitobah by its chief organizer, Thomas Spence) had collapsed in the face of company and British opposition, abetted by local recalcitrance. Lawlessness was dealt with by self-help, or not at all. Although the wearing of side-arms was not generally as common in the British territories as it was in the American frontier settlements, it was a regular practice in Portage la Prairie. When members of the McLean family and their neighbors left their homes, they were often armed.

One day in May, 1868, John McLean was planting potatoes, assisted by his adult children, Alex and Clementina. Not far away were tents belonging to some transient Métis traders. From the direction of the tents ran a terrified young woman, pursued by a drunken man brandishing a knife. The woman approached Clementina McLean, pleading for protection. Clementina recognized the pursuer as Francis Demarrais, a spirited individual with a reputation for being mean and dangerous when drunk. She warned him that she had a revolver, and would use it if he did not leave the woman alone. Apparently realizing that the formidable young lady usually meant what she said, Demarrais relented. He did not leave, however, but turned instead on the father, John McLean, who was working in another part of the field.

After delivering a barrage of taunts and threats which McLean tried to ignore, Demarrais deliberately dumped a sack of seed potatoes on the ground. McLean responded in some way that roused Demarrais to

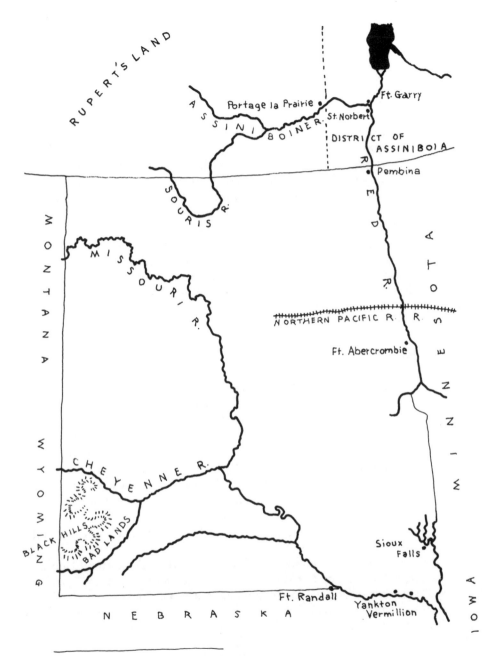

RUPERT'S LAND

ASSINIBOINER

Portage la Prairie

Ft. Garry

St. Norbert

DISTRICT OF ASSINIBOIA

SOURIS R.

Pembina

RED R.

MONTANA

MISSOURI R.

NORTHERN PACIFIC R. R.

Ft. Abercrombie

DAKOTA

MINNESOTA

WYOMING

CHEYENNE R.

BLACK HILLS   BAD LANDS

Sioux Falls

Ft. Randall

Yankton
Vermillion

IOWA

NEBRASKA

  DAKOTA TERRITORY
AND
RUPERT'S LAND
1868

N.S.

a frenzy of fury. One writer says McLean knocked him to the ground and disarmed him, throwing the knife into a nearby marsh.[2] The enraged Demarrais then ran to a neighboring farm, borrowed a shotgun, and rushed back to the McLean property. As he ran past one witness, William Garrioch, he let out what was described as a "war whoop."

Arriving at the McLean home, to which his adversary had withdrawn, Demarrais fired a shot in the direction of the door. He then turned and began to run away. An answering shot was heard from the direction of the house. Up to this point no blood had been spilled, but, as Demarrais continued his retreat, a third shot rang out, and he fell, severely wounded in the back. When William Garrioch arrived at the scene he saw Alex McLean, John's son, standing beside Demarrais. The injured man seemed to be paralyzed from the waist down. Garrioch heard Alex tell Demarrais: "If you had shot my father I would have shot you in the head, but since you didn't I just shot you in the back."[3]

Demarrais lived for another two months, but finally died in late July. Many local residents, especially in the Métis community, thought that Alex McLean had been criminally culpable. They regarded the shooting as altogether unnecessary in light of the fact that Demarrais had been in full retreat. Others were of the view that young McLean had acted justifiably. To settle the issue a trial would be necessary. The problem was that Portage la Prairie had no law enforcement machinery, and no court. Citizens of the settlement therefore petitioned the Council of Assiniboia to authorize its court to assume jurisdiction over the case. Although its legal authority to do so was dubious, the council complied with the request.[4] A grand jury was constituted, which indicted Alex McLean for manslaughter, and a special session of the Quarterly Court of Assiniboia was scheduled to hear the case August 24.

The McLean family was determined that Alex should be competently defended at the trial, but there were no trained lawyers in that part of British North America. Although "defence counsel" occasionally appeared before the Quarterly Court of Assiniboia, they were almost always just friends of the accused, unskilled in the law, whose only forensic weapons were compassion and common sense. The only fully qualified practicing lawyer within 500 miles of Winnipeg was Enos Stutsman, at Pembina. Stutsman was reasonably well known in the British territory, by reputation at least, from both the accounts of traders who passed through Pembina, and his own occasional visits to Winnipeg. The McLeans decided to retain him for Alex's defence.

Stutsman was well qualified for the assignment. While it may seem odd that a lawyer educated and experienced in the legal system of one country could function effectively in that of another, it must be remembered that the common law of England, which applied in British North America, was also the basis of the American legal system. Stutsman was not as experienced a court-room lawyer as he represented himself to be. At one point in the trial he stated in the court that he had had "considerable practice before the American courts, extending over a number of years."[5] It is doubtful, however, that he had been involved in any court case since moving to Pembina, or that his practice had ever been very extensive, even in his Sioux City days. There is certainly no evidence that he had ever undertaken a case as serious as this. Nevertheless, he seems always to have regarded himself as a lawyer first and foremost. He consistently described himself as such in the legislative records. Although he was absent in Pembina when the first Bar Association for the Territory was formed in Yankton in December 1866,[6] he was active in the affairs of the organization thereafter, and was a member of the committee formed in December 1867 to draft rules of practice for the Supreme Court of the Territory.[7] The McLean case would demonstrate that his powers of advocacy, regularly honed in the Legislative Assembly if not in the courtroom, were as keen as any client has a right to expect from a lawyer.

Stutsman's first advice to his client would be regarded by most modern practitioners as unethical: to flee the jurisdiction. On the day appointed for the trial, Stutsman appeared in court without the accused, and calmly explained that he had counselled his client to absent himself "for the time being." This advice, he told the astonished court, was based on his conviction that: "at this time there is an almost universal sentiment of prejudice against the defendant, which would operate materially against my client." The purpose of the advice was not to evade a trial, he said, but merely to delay it in order that the prejudice "might be allowed to die away." His client would be willing to appear if the hearing were postponed for a month.[8]

What difference would a month make? Although Stutsman did not say so openly, everyone in the courtroom would have been aware that in the intervening month the bulk of the Métis residents, who constituted by far the largest proportion of the population, and who were generally sympathetic to Demarrais, would have left the settlement for the fall buffalo hunt. The court lacked an effective constabulary to protect its proceedings, and there had been instances in the past of mob violence or intimidation interfering with its deliberations.[9] Stutsman's delaying tactic, while it would be unacceptable today, and was at least unorthodox at the time, was probably a justifiable expedient in a situation where lynch law was more to be feared than Her Majesty's writ. The court reprimanded Stutsman – though not severely. He apologized, stating rather unctuously that he would not have given the advice if he had known as much about the people and the courts of the area as he then did. The request adjournment was then granted – until September 25. The court even agreed that the bail bonds that had been put up by McLean and his father should not be forfeited. When the court reconvened, a month later, the accused was on hand.

The McLean case permits us to observe Enos Stutsman in action and to assess his prowess as an advocate. It also reveals much about the shortcomings of Assiniboia's judicial system.

The most fundamental flaw was the absence of sufficient law enforcement personnel. Most potential lawbreakers knew that the court's authority was hollow. And although many complaints had been registered with the company and with the British Government, nothing had been done to improve the situation. Hudson's Bay Company rule had entered a twilight stage. After almost two centuries of suzerainty, during the final fifty years of which its charter had been under constant legal and political attack, the company was now aware that it would soon be forced to surrender both ownership and governmental responsibility to the new confederation of British North

American colonies known as Canada. Its chief concern at this stage was with the amount of compensation that would be paid in return for this gigantic land transfer. The adequacy of the interim governmental arrangements for the area was a matter of little interest to the company, and no suggestion for improvement was likely to be given serious consideration if it would involve additional expense. British authorities, anxious to turn over full responsibility to Canada as quickly as possible, displayed a similar indifference.

The principal judge of the Quarterly Court of Assiniboia, John Black,[10] also left something to be desired. He was a good-hearted and generally fair-minded individual, a trifle pompous but well-intentioned. But neither his Scottish training as a solicitor, nor his previous employment, as a young man in the fur trade, or later, in Australian government service, had equipped him properly for the job. He lacked a sound understanding of court procedure, and, in view of the absence of an effective police force to support his edicts, he tended to avoid confrontation. When unopposed in the courtroom, he was sometimes capable of administering justice tempered by wise discretion, but he could be made to seem bumbling and indecisive by a professional advocate as skilled as Enos Stutsman.

The opening of the trial was low key. The newspaper described it sarcastically: "Her maj – no, the Honorable Company's court was opened by the Chief Justice, who *acting as crier* for the occasion, used the following formula: 'Well, the hour is getting late, let us proceed to business...' "[11] John Black, whose formal title was Recorder of Rupert's Land, but who was usually referred to as "Judge" or "Chief Justice," was assisted, usually in silence, by three magistrates. The fourth magistrate on the normally five-man court was acting as sheriff for the day due to the temporary absence of the regular sheriff.

After recounting the circumstances relating to the postponement of the trial, Judge Black called for the indictment to be read, and asked the accused whether he pleaded guilty or not guilty. At that point the judge's first run-in with Stutsman occurred. The latter stood (no taller standing behind the little counsel table than when seated) and said, "We shall enter the usual plea of not guilty." The judge replied, curtly, "It is usual for the prisoner to plead for himself," and again asked

14. Judge John Black

McLean to speak. Then followed a lengthy wrangle in which Stutsman demanded, and eventually won, the right to enter plea for his client. It was a minor victory, but one which gave the accused a psychological advantage. The court had been put on the defensive. Stutsman had served notice that he would be vigilant in the enforcement of his client's every right.

The next point of dispute was of much greater substance, and called for considerable tact on Stutsman's part. A twelve-man jury was empanelled, consisting, as had been the practice for many years in the ethnically bifurcated community, of six who were primarily French speaking, and six who had English or Scottish backgrounds. Stutsman was concerned that some of the French-speaking jurors would not be able to understand his arguments. On the other hand, most of them were Métis who had not joined the buffalo hunt, and he knew he could not afford to alienate Métis opinion in a case that already had dangerous ethnic undertones. He politely requested leave to address the court concerning the composition of the jury, and made the following carefully chosen remarks:

While I have no prejudice on account of blood or race – none whatever – I have a strong objection to having the case tried before those gentlemen in the jury box if there be any of them who do not understand the English language. I can only address the jury in English; and as it will be important that they should thoroughly understand the whole of my argument, it will be as necessary that they should also be conversant with the English tongue.

In looking at the gentlemen of the jury I can see none of whom I should wish out of the box on any other grounds. I would as lief they were every one of them of French extraction as not, providing they could all of them understand what I shall have to say to them. I see many intelligent faces among these gentlemen, but am personally acquainted with but two or three of them. If there are any gentlemen among them who will not be able to understand me, I would desire that he be so removed, and replaced by some other one who will understand English. I believe that throughout the length and breadth of the British dominions the English tongue is the only legal language in which to transact legal business.[12]

Judge Black suggested that the difficulty could be overcome, as it always had been in the past, by the use of an interpreter. However, after Stutsman explained why such a procedure would be awkward and unsatisfactory, the judge relented and asked a French-speaking magistrate to request any members of the jury who had not understood the lawyer's remarks to withdraw. Two did so, and were replaced by Métis familiar with English. A risky maneuver had been executed skillfully and successfully.

As soon as the jury had been sworn in, Stutsman was on his crutches again, pointing out that since some of the testimony would probably be in French, it would still be necessary for the court to appoint an interpreter for the benefit of himself and those members of the bench and the jury who did not understand French. The person he suggested for the job, and whom the court agreed to appoint, was none other than Stutsman's Pembina crony, Joe Rolette. Whether it was the father or the son is not clear, but to have brought along either man was an inspired touch on Stutsman's part. Many interpreters would have been available at Red River, but few whom he could be sure to be wholly free of bias. More important, both the senior and junior Rolettes were well respected by the Assiniboia Métis, and the presence of either man would exert a restraining influence against any impulse to invoke lynch law.

The court was now ready to hear the evidence for the prosecution. There was no prosecuting attorney, however. Judge Black had been accustomed to playing that role. He would first outline the Crown's theory of the case to the jury, and then question the witnesses for the prosecution. This procedure, similar to that which was and still is followed in many "civil law" jurisdictions, differed radically from the common law procedure with which Stutsman was familiar, and which was also applicable in Assiniboia. By the common-law method, usually described as "adversarial," the court remains aloof from the presentation of evidence pro or con, leaving that task to counsel for the prosecution and the defence respectively. When Judge Black announced that he would now "proceed to lay the case before the jury" in the manner customary in that court, Stutsman leaped up, and the following exchange ensued:

STUTSMAN

I beg to remonstrate and protest against... proceeding (in that fashion). I have had considerable experience in the practice of law, and I have never seen a judge acting as Crown attorney. I... (suggest that) the Court... appoint someone else as Crown prosecutor. Between opposing attorneys there often arise points of law which require argument, and have to be referred to the bench for final decision. If Your Honor acts as Crown attorney, how can I call upon you as judge to reverse your own decision in case it should be necessary? How could Your Honor, for instance, consistently argue on a question of your own propounding?

I hope that Your Honor will not place yourself in such an anomalous position, but will appoint someone else to examine the witnesses.

BLACK

I feel that I came prepared to deal justly in this case, as in every other, and I think that I can act properly! I admit that my position is a peculiar one – and also very embarrassing – but inasmuch as it has been the usual course of procedure... (here), I will proceed to address the jury.

(To the jury:) The Prisoner Alexander McLean is brought before you for killing Francis Demarrais under circumstances amounting to manslaughter...

Stutsman refused to be silenced, and interjected:

STUTSMAN

I beg Your Honor's pardon for interrupting, but I would like to know if the Court intends to examine the witnesses for the prosecution. Will you leave the witnesses to tell their own story – simply their own unvarnished tale, or do you intend to prompt the witnesses by leading questions?

BLACK

The witnesses may tell their own stories as they please.

STUTSMAN

I still object strongly to Your Honor's examining the witnesses. On a disputed point of law I could not think of asking the associate judges to condemn their head!

At this point the judge began to retreat.

BLACK

Have you an objection to my asking *any* questions?

STUTSMAN

No Your Honor. The Court has the right to ask a witness for information upon evidence it does not understand, but it has no right to prompt evidence by asking new and leading questions. It may only ask for information upon evidence already before the Court.

Judge Black then conceded victory to the persistent counsel, ordering that the court clerk, Mr. W.R. Smith, should act as prosecuting attorney. This must have come as a shock to the unprepared Smith. He had learned in twenty years as clerk of the frontier court to take unexpected developments in his stride, but to have the prosecution of this very important case thrust on him at a moment's notice must have left him breathless. For Stutsman it was a great tactical victory – perhaps the crucial one – for an unprepared Smith would be a much less formidable adversary than the well-briefed judge.

The first prosecution witness was William Garrioch, who had seen the latter part of the tragedy unfold. He confirmed that Demarrais had been drunk, had fired a shotgun toward the McLean house, and had been fleeing when felled by the second of two shots from the vicinity of the house. He could not say who had fired the latter shots, but he testified to having overheard Alex McLean tell Demarrais as he lay on the ground that he had done so, and would have shot him in the head if the elder McLean had been injured. The latter statement was the most damning evidence Stutsman had to deal with, and he was unsuccessful in shaking Garrioch's recollection on cross-examination. He did however, extract the useful information that on the day before his death Demarrais had been seen to have a second serious wound, unrelated to the spinal injury. He also had the witness confirm that Demarrais was sometimes "a devil" when drunk.

As Garrioch left the stand, Prosecutor Smith was in a quandary as to how to proceed. Several other prosecution witnesses had been scheduled, but none had appeared. One was at Poplar Point, ill and without suitable transportation. Another was in the United States on a trading mission. (Special Agent Stutsman provoked laughter at this point by commenting that the witness would forfeit more than his subpoena bond if apprehended by United States Customs officials.) The third, a young woman, was convalescing from a recent childbirth.

Judge Black, reverting to his accustomed role as director of the prosecution, decided to fill the gaps in the Crown's case by calling the accused's father, John McLean, to the witness stand. This posed a serious threat to the defence, because the elder McLean had presumably seen Alex shoot Demarrais, and may have been unwilling to perjure himself, even to save his son from conviction.

Stutsman was equal to the occasion. It required lengthy argument, of a legally dubious nature, to accomplish his purpose, however. The thrust of his argument can be seen from the following passage:

It is with great reluctance that I beg to protest against John McLean being called as a witness for the Crown. The Court has extended many favors toward me, and on that account I have refrained from objecting to many – very many – informalities I have noticed in the general proceedings of the Court.

During the sitting of the Grand Jury, I sent Mr. John McLean to the Court that he might ask the Court if his testimony would be required before the Grand Jury, and he was not allowed to appear before that body. Consequently, I cannot allow him to be used as a Crown witness at this stage of the proceedings...

According to the common-law of England it is the rule that the names of the witnesses examined before the Grand Jury, on the strength of whose testimony the Grand Jury brought in their indictment, should be endorsed on the back of the indictment, and a copy of that instrument, together with a copy of the testimony upon which that body acted is always given to the attorney for the defence. It is of the utmost importance that the defence should know the testimony against which they will have to contend, else how can they be prepared to rebut false evidence? A witness may not be worthy of credence upon oath; he may be a perjurer, and what not. How can that be shown by the defense if they do not know who he is in time to prepare themselves?

This was a misrepresentation of the common law. The Crown was entitled to call to the stand any witness present in court other than the accused or his or her spouse, regardless of whether they had been examined by the grand jury or were listed on the indictment.[13] The argument sounded plausible, though, and the brilliant little defence lawyer had already seriously undermined the court's self-confidence. Judge Black did not give in easily, however. When he resisted Stutsman's submissions, the latter's voice rose to a pitch of insistence not previously heard during the trial:

...No court under heaven could make John McLean appear as a witness for the prosecution!...

(Referring to previously mentioned informalities that he had over-looked:) *I have waived a wrong; I now claim a right!* Grand Juries must examine the witnesses for the prosecution... They *must* – they *must* – have the testimony of the witnesses, and they *must* endorse the names of those witnesses upon the back of the indictment. This is a plain common sense view of the matter, and fairness and common sense are the principles of English law...

Every man is innocent until proved to be guilty. Does the Court *want to prove* the prisoner guilty... ?

If the Court bring John McLean into the box as evidence for the Crown, it can, by shaping its questions, bring out everything it may wish; but if the defence bring him into the witness stand the Court can only cross examine him as to the questions which he – the counsel – has already asked.

Again, this misdescribes the true limits of cross-examination, but Stutsman had again beaten the court into submission. Seizing as a face-saving device what he construed as a promise by Stutsman to call McLean as a defence witness, Judge Black ruled that he could not be heard as a prosecution witness because he was not listed on the indictment.

Smith was about to close the Crown's case for lack of further evidence when a young woman named Marie Blondin appeared at the courthouse door. She was the witness who had been reported confined to bed due to childbirth. She announced that she was willing to testify in spite of her weakened condition. After being sworn, she told the court, through interpreter Rolette, about seeing Demarrais assault a young woman and pursue her to the McLean farm on the day of the shooting, about the altercation between Demarrais and John McLean, culminating in Demarrais's firing of the shotgun, and about seeing Demarrais shot in the back. At this point a juror asked the witness the vital question: "Who fired the shot?"

Before she could reply, Stutsman objected vociferously to the question. He had been astute enough at the beginning of her testimony to get a ruling from the court, after another legal debate, that jurors could not ask questions. Now he sought to apply that ruling to the most potentially damaging question of the day. As Judge Black once more attempted to resist the lawyer's submission, a juryman interjected: "Thus far no case has been made out, and I think I speak for my brother jurymen as well as for myself in saying that." His point seems to have been that in view of the ineffectual presentation of the prosecution's case, the jury must be allowed to ask questions if the facts were ever to emerge. The defence attorney must have been delighted by this confirmation that his tactics were succeeding. He would also have been pleased to hear the judge reprimand the juryman and thereby widen the gulf between the jury and the bench.

Eventually, however, Judge Black intimated that the juror's question was admissible. Stutsman, knowing he had the court on the run, then resorted to exasperation: "Your Honor, how long is this thing to keep on?" In the end, as on all the previous matters, he won his point. The question was excluded. Why Prosecutor Smith did not then repeat the juror's question as his own is not clear. Perhaps he had already closed the Crown's case before the question was asked, or perhaps he was simply flustered by the high-powered tactics of his foxy opponent. Stutsman seems to have waived cross-examination, probably to get the witness out of the box as quickly as possible.

It was now time for the defence to present its evidence, but there was little need to do so; as the outspoken juror had indicated, there was not much of a case to meet. Stutsman contented himself with calling another character witness, who testified that he "would as lief meet a mad buffalo bull as Francis Demarrais when drunk." He then informed the court: "Your Honor, here I rest my case."

This caused some consternation on the bench:

BLACK
Mr. Stutsman, I understood you to say that you would call Mr. John McLean to the witness stand, but you have failed to do so.

STUTSMAN
I see no necessity of doing so, as the prosecution has failed to make out a point against my client. Had there been any evidence given on the part of the Crown that it would have been necessary to rebut I would have been perfectly prepared to (call Mr. McLean), but it is totally unnecessary to bring any rebutting testimony in the way the case now stands.

The newspaper account commented that the defence counsel had promised to call the witness and allow the judge to cross-examine him, but its own report of that portion of the trial indicates that Stutsman had been careful to avoid giving such an undertaking explicitly. He undoubtedly knew that Judge Black thought he had given an undertaking, of course. In any event, McLean was not forced to take the stand, and the trial moved on to the stage of addresses to the jury.

Mr. Smith, who had clearly had his fill of impromptu lawyering, declined to make any remarks. Enos Stutsman spoke at length. Although the newspaper report of his speech is severely truncated, enough is reported to show that he employed both charm and logic to full effect. First came a characteristic apology:

I beg the pardon of the Court for any disrespectful language I may have used. I may have spoken more in the heat of the moment than I had intended, but, of course, as I am in duty bound, I had the interest and welfare of my client at heart. I may occasionally have transgressed the bounds of true courtesy. If I have done so, I ask the pardon of this honorable Court.

Then he dealt with the evidence, contending first that there was no proof as to who shot Demarrais. This was not quite correct, of course; William Garrioch had testified to hearing Alex McLean admit the shooting. Stutsman no doubt stressed the danger of relying on such second-hand evidence, the meaning of which could be entirely altered by one or two words being misunderstood in the pressure of the circumstances. Secondly, he argued, it had not been proved that Demarrais's death on July 26 had been caused by the shot fired in May. There was evidence of some other injury having been sustained by Demarrais in unknown circumstances. This or other undisclosed events could possibly have caused the death. Finally, even if it had been shown that Demarrais died as a result of a shot fired by the accused, Stutsman contended, the shot would have been a justifiable act of self-defence and family protection in the face of a vicious attack by a dangerous and irrational person.[14] Although the newspaper account did not refer to it, his address would certainly have ended with an emotional peroration about not punishing a fine young man for acting loyally and courageously in time of great peril to his family.

Judge Black was probably sympathetic to Alex McLean, but he must have been frustrated at seeing the prosecution's case so inadequately presented, and at having been so frequently humiliated before the leaders of the community by this clever man from south of the border. Whatever the reasons, his summation to the jury sounded like a prosecutor's harangue. As Stutsman no doubt knew, this approach was more likely to assist the defence than if he had striven for an appearance of impartiality, and the defence attorney took advantage of every opportunity to stress the judge's bias, interrupting the summation frequently, and (ignoring his earlier pious apology) drawing Black into quarrel after quarrel.

It took the jury only ten minutes to acquit Alex McLean. Stutsman claimed that they deliberated for even less time than that. In a letter to Governor Faulk on September 28, he said:

Your kind letter... was received last evening on my arrival home from Fort Garry – British Red River Settlement – where I defended and cleared a young man on trial for killing a French half breed. This is the first case I have conducted in the Queen's Court, and the perfect success was far more grattifying (sic) to me than was the $100 fee (gold). The jury retired and within 3 minutes returned a verdict of "not guilty". I left for home well pleased with British juries, and not at al (sic) displeased with myself![15]

He had good reason to be pleased with himself. The case against his client had been strong: all accounts of the incident indicate that Alex McLean fired the shot that felled Francis Demarrais, that the latter had been in full retreat at the time, and that he had been immobilized in bed in steadily deteriorating condition from then until the day of the death.[16] While it is not very difficult for a lawyer of even middling competence to tie knots in a legal proceeding if there are no other lawyers on the scene, it must be remembered that Stutsman faced two special problems in this case. First, the court was a power unto itself, being responsible to no higher court of appeal. Second, the passions of the Métis community (the large majority of the total population) had been aroused against his client, and the court had no adequate means of protection against mob action. While the majority of the Métis were absent, there were still sufficient numbers

93

A Special Court held on the 25th Sept. 1868 - Judge Black

The Queen } For manslaughter, being charged on an Indictment
versus } with having on the 23rd of June 1868, at Portage la
Wm McLean } prairie shot one Baptiste Demarais, who died of
the wound caused by the shot on the 26th July 1868
- To the Charge the prisoner pleaded "Not Guilty"

— For the Prosecution —

Wm Garrioch, Sworn, — Early in the summer I saw Demarais
he was in drink - while trying to get into a cart he
fell back on the road, I passed on to McLean's and
returned with Wm Gaddy - I left him at Gaddy's
bye next to McLean's house. The man came
running towards Gaddy's house - I cannot say
he went into the house - In a short time he
returned with a double-barrel Gun - I wanted to
stop him, but he ran till he came opposite to
McLean's door - He came to a dead stand and
fired a shot towards the door - immediately after
firing he ran off again - He ran but a few steps
when I heard two shots fired from the house - after
a short time a third shot was fired and Demarais
fell - I heard John McLean talking loud to Gaddy
- I heard him accuse Gaddy of being the cause of
Demarais shooting at him - I saw the prisoner, who
said "If he had shot my father I would have shot
him in the head but, as he did not I shot him in
the back" - I had the Gun in my hand and
the deceased said "There is no use I will do no more
harm" - I do not believe he had the Gun to his
shoulder - I saw the man who shot him but could
not say who it was - I thought it was the prisoner
but would not swear to it.

141

... Deceased caught hold of a woman ...
and fell over the fence - It was in the woo...
wanted to pull up her clothes, he had a knif...
...te, she got up to McLean's house and the
... was there before her - when we got up to the
... McLean told me not to be afraid, that she ha...
. McLean was planting potatoes and deceased
...ag and danced about - Deceased wanted to speak
... but McLean did not listen to him - I heard
...ts and the prisoner said "Demarais is gone for
... - After I went back I found Demarais lying
...ound asking pardon of Mrs McLean, who said
...ot shake hands with a dog - They put him in a
... dragged him away.—

— For the Defence —
... — I dwell at the Settlement - I knew
...ais, - when sober he was quiet and decent
...en drunk was a devil - when in that state
...d as soon meet a hostile Sioup as him —

Verdict — "Not Guilty"

15. Record, Quarterly Court of Assiniboia, September 28, 1868

in the area to constitute a threat if they decided to act in concert. To have won every procedural dispute with the judge, and then to have convinced a racially divided jury to return what must have been a unanimous verdict without significant deliberation was a feat of which lawyers much more experienced than Enos Stutsman would have been justly proud. A few months later the *Nor'Wester* contained the following item:

NEWS!!

We have been out in search of news and learn the following: That his Honor Judge Black is shortly to be superceded, and that the Hon. Enos Stuttman (sic) is to be appointed Chief Justice in his place.[17]

Although it was probably intended as a joke, it is an eloquent comment on the settlement's assessment of Stutsman's performance.

The McLean family was doubtless satisfied that they had received full value for their $100 fee. They may also have been more than a little surprised at the result. They seem to have been prepared for a contrary verdict. An early history of Manitoba claims that both the prisoner and a number of his friends in the courtroom were well armed, that a saddled horse was being held in readiness just outside the building, and that the redoubtable Clementina McLean sat throughout the trial with her back against the open door so that it could not be closed to prevent a quick escape.[18]

The McLean case seems to have been only the second one in which a fully qualified lawyer appeared before the courts of Assiniboia.[19] It was certainly the first in which the colony's primitive legal procedures were subjected to such excoriating criticism. The inadequacies of the judicial system had been under attack for some time,[20] and the McLean case provided critics with abundant additional ammunition. One of the jurors later described the case as a "memorable pantomime" in a letter to the *Nor'Wester*,[21] and the editor of that newspaper referred to it as a "farcical burlesque" in an article listing all the procedural faults Stutsman had exposed.[22] The *Nor'Wester's* editor was a consistent critic of almost everything associated with the company, of course, but it is probable that a large percentage of Assiniboia residents shared his sentiments when he wrote: "We never in our life saw so much controversy in a court of Justice between a Judge and a member of the bar. Identified, as we desire to be, with the fortunes of this country, we felt ashamed and sorry for the honor of British law and Justice."[23] What the writer may not have fully appreciated was that, while many of the spats between Stutsman and Black were legitimate, he had also witnessed a consummate display of the time-honored forensic art of judge baiting.

Judge John Black should not be criticized too severely. Although he had been irresolute to the point of low comedy, and had permitted himself to be forced into a prosecutorial stance, both shortcomings were rooted in the legal system itself. It was not easy to be resolute in face of the knowledge that neither the company nor the British Government was entirely confident as to the legality of the charter from which his powers derived,[24] and that neither was willing to provide law enforcement facilities adequate to prevent his rulings being blithely ignored by any determined group that chose to do so. His use of the "inquisitorial" style of criminal proceeding was probably justifiable, if not unavoidable, in a community without lawyers. His interventions on behalf of the Crown to compensate for the disparity in prowess and preparedness between Stutsman and Smith, were well-intentioned, if misguided. To be effective, an adversarial system of litigation requires that the advocates of opposing interests be relatively well-matched. The sudden injection of someone like Stutsman into a previously lawyerless system, without a comparably skilled advocate on the other side, was bound to throw the system out of kilter.

The trial made Stutsman an instant celebrity in the British settlement. Although it is clear from his letter to Faulk three days later that he intended to exploit this fact, and would "probably spend much of my time on the British side of the line,"[25] he could not have known how intimately – and how soon – his personal fortunes would be intertwined with those of the restless northern colony.

CHAPTER FIVE

THE RIEL REBELLION
1869-1870

EVERYONE KNEW THAT THE HUDSON'S BAY
Company's two-hundred-year reign over Rupert's Land would
soon be over. As early as 1857, a British parliamentary committee had recommended that the vast area drained by Hudson Bay,
ceded to the company in 1670, be re-organized, and that company
rule be ended in areas of actual or potential settlement.[1] Although the
implementation of that recommendation had been held up for many
years by more pressing matters, it was obvious that it could not be
delayed much longer.

Almost every aspect of Hudson's Bay Company government was
unsatisfactory. When, for example, Enos Stutsman had complained in
a letter to the Winnipeg newspaper *The Nor'Wester* about the inade-
quacy of the postal service, he was strongly supported by an editorial
comment.[2] The weakness of the judicial system, as demonstrated by
the McLean case, had been the cause of renewed criticism of company
rule.[3] Even one of the jurors in the case had complained.[4] When the
newspaper reported Stutsman's attempt to establish female suffrage in

Dakota, it was with a wry local allusion:

We see by our exchanges that the Hon. Enos Stutsman has introduced a bill in the Dakota legislature which, if passed, will confer the elective franchise upon women.

It would be something remarkable if our nearest neighbours should allow female suffrage, whilst in this country even the men are not allowed to vote. Verily, this is a land of progress.[5]

The question remaining to be answered was what form a new governmental organization should take. Three very different solutions were possible, and each had its advocates. Some called for the establishment of new Crown colony in the area. However, the principal British North American colonies had just amalgamated as the new Dominion of Canada, and the Canadian Government was actively seeking the absorption of all remaining British territories on the continent, including Rupert's Land. A relatively small but vociferous and   expanding group of newcomers from the new Province of Ontario was campaigning within the settlement for this same goal. Finally, there was a smaller but equally active enclave of Americans – hotel-keepers and other businessmen in the burgeoning town of Winnipeg – who sought annexation of the territory by the United States.

If the annexation option had drawn its sole support from the Yankees who gathered nightly at O'Lone's Red Saloon and Dutch George Emmerling's hotel in Winnipeg, it could have been safely discounted. There was, however, a sufficiently long history of official American interest in Rupert's Land to make the idea seem a plausible alternative. James Wickes Taylor of St. Paul, Minnesota, who was destined for a long and distinguished career as United States consul at Winnipeg, had been commissioned by the United States Government in 1859 to report on conditions in Rupert's Land and other British American territories. His scholarly communiques provided Washington a more revealing window on affairs in the Hudson's Bay country than was likely available in either London or other British possessions.[6] In 1861 Abraham Lincoln's secretary of state, William Seward, had made a speech in St. Paul which left no doubt as to his belief that

America's "manifest destiny" included the extension of its boundaries north of the 49th parallel.[7]

Mr. Seward may have been encouraged to announce his expansionist ambitions by statements Taylor had been clipping from the Winnipeg *Nor'Wester* to the effect that "... the people of Red River are becoming indifferent to the British connection... They would bear a severance without regret,"[8] and that there was, even as early as 1860, a growing "feeling in favour of the U.S.A...."[9] In 1866 a House of Representatives' bill, drafted with the assistance of J.W. Taylor, presumptuously called for the admission of all British North American possessions into the American union.[10] That measure was not treated very seriously, but British and Canadian leaders found ample cause for concern in 1867 (the same year the Dominion of Canada was created) when Secretary Seward announced, "I know that Nature designs that this whole continent, not merely these thirty-six states, shall be sooner or later within the magic circle of the American union".[11] Seward was speaking in generalities, of course, and perhaps with distant time horizons in mind, but his acquisition of Alaska for the United States that same year left little doubt as to his earnestness.

Other American politicians, especially those from the lusty young state of Minnesota, were even less patient than Seward was in their desire to acquire the Hudson's Bay country. Early in 1868 the Minnesota Legislature passed a resolution calling on Congress to annex the territory between Alaska and the United States proper. When the *Nor'Wester* reported this resolution it commented that nine-tenths of the local population would prefer annexation by the United States if there were to be a change of status. This opinion was quickly picked up by the St. Paul *Daily Press*, and passed on to Washington by J.W. Taylor.[12] Taylor had observed in an earlier report that, "We have only to deposit an 'open basket'... under the tree and the ripe fruit will speedily fall."[13]

Senator Alexander Ramsey from Minnesota was particularly enthusiastic about annexation. It was on his initiative that a United States consulate was established in Winnipeg in the summer of 1869,[14] staffed by his friend and even more avid annexationist Oscar

Malmros. When Ramsey then proposed that an American general be authorized to lead an expedition of exploration through the British North American northwest,[15] Seward's department had to explain, rather curtly, that such an enterprise "could certainly not... be undertaken by officers in the service of the United States, without the permission of the British Government, which, under existing circumstances, it is not deemed advisable to request."[16] The "circumstances" referred to were the still strained relations between the United States and Great Britain resulting from the latter's apparent friendliness to the Confederate States during the Civil War. They were circumstances which also served to whet American appetites for the annexation of Rupert's Land.

Enos Stutsman was fully aware of both the possibility of annexation and the opportunities it would offer to Americans who were on the scene early. During the closing stages of the McLean trial, in response to an accusation by Judge Black that he was injecting politics into some of his remarks, Stutsman claimed to support the political *status quo* in Rupert's Land, but his voice must have been heavy with sarcasm:

No, Your Honor, far from it. I should be sorry to have you labor under any such impression. I do think that if these people want any change, or a government other than the one they have that they are the greatest fools living. And so are those who talk about annexation to any other country. Why, what do they want? (They) can do as they please, and no taxes! Why, Sir, I think if this people with their blue beans and hominy cannot be happy here, they would not be in Paradise![17]

The spectators in the courtroom burst into laughter, and Stutsman knew he had struck a responsive chord. Two days later, when he wrote to Governor Faulk to tell him about the trial and to announce that in light of the prevailing confusion in Dakota politics, he intended to "retire to private life and see if I cannot make an honest living," he remarked:

I shall probably spend much of my time on the British side of the line – and if Uncle Sam purchases or gobbles them, I will come in *with* them.[18]

As he had at Yankton, he intended to arrive before the rush.

By far the largest segment of the Rupert's Land population was composed of French-speaking Métis. Although they were generally dissatisfied with company rule, the Métis were, as a group, much less precise about the settlements' political future than were the resident Americans, Canadian Scottish–English, or the Scottish–Indian mixed blood populations. Yet, paradoxically, it was the Métis community that provided the leadership and power which ultimately settled the question.

When it was learned in Rupert's Land that negotiations were in progress in London between representatives of the Hudson's Bay Company and the British and Canadian governments, with a view to transferring sovereignty over the territory to Canada, the local Canadians were overjoyed, but most of the other residents were suspicious or irate. They spoke angrily of being sold to Canada "like a flock of sheep"[19] for the £300,000 transfer price, and they resented not being consulted about the terms of the transfer or about the form of government that would replace company rule.

The Métis had, in addition to this general dissatisfaction, some particular concerns, relating to the preservation of their culture and lifestyle. As French-speaking Roman Catholics, they feared what would happen if the Canadians, most of whose local representatives were linguistically bigotted and militantly "anti-Papist," controlled the reins of government. They also worried about their land holdings. Due to the absence of a satisfactory registration system, their title to land had never been formally acknowledged. The boundaries of their plots were vaguely defined, and the land was often left uninhabited while the owners were on the plains hunting buffalo or engaging in trade. Their property would therefore be tempting targets for the land-hungry Canadian and American newcomers. Métis suspicions intensified when, in the fall of 1868, a small survey crew was sent prematurely by the Canadian government to the yet-to-be-transferred territory. Although that survey did not directly affect any Métis land interests, the unruly and stridently pro-Canadian complexion of the crew was disturbing. The size of the survey operations expanded in the summer of 1869, and as they began to approach Métis-occupied land, concern increased.

16. William McDougall

At about the same time, news reached the settlement that the Canadian Government had chosen a man to be Governor of the territory. He was William McDougall, who had been one of Canada's representatives at the London negotiations, and who, as Canadian Minister of Public Works, had been responsible for sending out the first survey teams. Although the formal transfer of jurisdiction to Canada had not yet taken place, McDougall was to be dispatched to Winnipeg early, in order to be on the scene when the transfer occurred.

What was most distressing about this news was the fact that the government McDougall was instructed to put in place was not a representative democracy like those which functioned in each of the Canadian provinces, but an appointive administration controlled by the governor on instructions from Ottawa. The area was not to become a province, but would have only territorial status, for the time being, at least. Travelling with McDougall would be a retinue of Canadian "carpet-baggers," who were to form the nucleus of the new government, and it was obvious that the lion's share of the remaining appointments would be made from the ranks of resident Canadians. The leader of Winnipeg's Canadians, Dr. John Schultz, had recommended, in a letter to McDougall's brother earlier in the year, precisely the form of government that was to be established.[20] The Métis were all too aware that the proposed arrangement would enable a small and intolerant segment of the community to impose its will on the majority.

After a summer of rather unfocussed grumbling, punctuated by occasional episodes of suspected claim-jumpers being warned off Métis land, the Métis leaders began to organize a more coordinated resistance in the early autumn of 1869. A committee was formed, consisting of elected representatives from every Métis parish. This group held a series of meetings at St. Norbert in August and September to decide what action to take. Prominent at these meetings was 24-year old Louis Riel, who had recently returned to the settlement from a lengthy sojourn in Quebec and Minnesota.[21] The son of a once-prominent Métis leader, Riel was articulate and well educated; he was also passionately devoted to both his religion and the rights of the Métis people. This charismatic young man quickly emerged as the catalyst and principal spokesman for the dissident group. Another person who seems to have played an important role – in an advisory capacity – during at least some of these early strategy meetings was Enos Stutsman.[22]

In view of his role as successful defence counsel the previous fall in the McLean trial – a case interlaced with ethnic antipathy – it may seem surprising that the Métis leaders should have gone to Stutsman for advice. It must be borne in mind, however, that both the situation they faced and the measures they contemplated had significant legal dimensions. What was the legal position of unregistered land occupants, for instance? What right had Canadian surveyors to conduct their operations before the formal transfer of jurisdiction was complete? What measures could lawfully be taken against the governor-designate before that time? It is entirely understandable that when wrestling with these difficult legal questions Louis Riel and his colleagues should have decided to consult the only fully qualified practicing lawyer within five hundred miles. It should not be forgotten, either, that Stutsman was a good friend of the highly esteemed Rolette family, and might therefore have been more readily accepted by the Métis community than other English-speaking advisers.

By October 11, when the survey crew working its way northward from Pembina first entered land occupied by Métis residents, the discussions had reached a sufficiently advanced stage to permit a swift and firm response to be made. As the surveyors were conducting operations on the hay lands of André Nault, a group of Métis led by Louis Riel approached, stood defiantly on the survey chain, and demanded that the crew withdraw. Riel announced that the land south of the Assiniboine River belonged to the Métis people, not to Canada, and that the people had decided the survey should proceed no further. The demonstration succeeded in halting the survey operations. When Riel was called upon to explain the action to the company authorities to whom the chief surveyor complained, he was adamant in his insistence that only the people of the settlement had the right to decide how the land should be dealt with.

With this successful confrontation behind them, the committee was reorganized on a formal basis as the National Committee of the

17. Louis Riel and colleagues (probably National Committee of the Métis of Red River). Riel is seated in the center, with John Bruce on his right and W.B. O'Donoghue on his left.

Métis of Red River, with John Bruce as its nominal president and young Louis Riel as secretary and real leader. Attention was then directed to the Canadian governor-designate, William McDougall, whose party was approaching Pembina from the south. A barricade was erected across the Pembina trail at St. Norbert, and preparations were made to stop the vice-regal cavalcade at the international boundary.

When McDougall arrived at the United States Customs House in Pembina on October 31, he was met by a messenger from the Métis National Committee, who had been waiting there for three or four days. The messenger handed the prospective governor a letter and quickly disappeared. The letter, written in French, read as follows:

Dated at St. Norbert, Red River, this 21st day of October 1869.

Sir,

The National Committee of the Metis of Red River orders William McDougall not to enter the Territory of the North West without special permission of the above-mentioned committee.

By order of the President, John Bruce.

Louis Riel, Secretary,[23]

McDougall treated the ultimatum with the disdain he thought it deserved. After clearing United States Customs, he and his party crossed the border and proceeded as far as a Hudson's Bay Company post two miles north of Pembina. Here they received a message from the chief surveyor warning them of the seriousness of the Métis resistance. McDougall decided to send an envoy ahead, and to remain at the post until the situation was better known. He wrote a brief personal letter reporting the problem to Prime Minister John A. Macdonald that evening, and mentioned that "secret meetings" were going on in Pembina at the moment between the insurgents and local sympathizers (who certainly included Enos Stutsman). However, he assured Macdonald, "I am not frightened and don't believe the insurrection will last a week."[24]

McDougall's envoy was J.A.N. Provencher, a nephew of the first Bishop of the territory. It was thought that he would be trusted by the Métis. Another member of the McDougall party, an impetuous and not-too-astute young military officer named Captain Donald Cameron, also proceeded northward. Cameron was acting contrary to McDougall's wishes. He believed that he could put a stop to the rebel nonsense by displaying a firm military manner. Provencher met with Riel and his colleagues, and assisted at a church service for them, but he encountered firm, though polite, resistance to every suggestion that the governor's party should be allowed to proceed. Cameron, who rode imperiously up to the St. Norbert barricade and demanded, "Remove that blasted fence!" was treated equally firmly, and a good deal less politely. Neither diplomacy nor bluster could bend the Métis will. Both men were escorted back to the boundary.

In the meantime, the governor-designate was encountering difficulties of his own. No sooner had he decided to remain at the Hudson's Bay Company trading post than he was called upon by a Chippawa Indian chief, Kewetaosh, and a number of his councillors. Like the Métis messenger, Kewetaosh had been awaiting the party's arrival at Pembina for quite some time.[25] McDougall agreed to meet with the Indians the following morning, and did so as soon as he had sent Provencher on his way northward. After the customary pipe-smoking ritual, Kewetaosh announced that he was sorry to hear about the Métis uprising at the settlement and, in McDougall's words, "he wished me not to go there." McDougall chose to construe this as a "friendly warning." This was a reasonable interpretation in view of the chief's subsequent disclaimer that he or his band "had anything to to with the movements or designs of the French Half-Breeds." The major concern of Kewetaosh and his band was expressed in question form: Was it true that McDougall had purchased land which belonged to his tribe (the perimeters of which he described) from the Hudson's Bay Company? What would happen to the land under the new government? McDougall seems to have handled the meeting adroitly, assuring the chief that the change of administration would have no effect on Indian rights, whatever they might be, and agreeing to a conference to discuss those rights with Kewetaosh in the spring. The Indians appear to have left satisfied.[26]

Although McDougall did not realize it at the time, he had just experienced the first of numerous salvos fired in his direction during the next few weeks by Enos Stutsman. The Indians probably came to Pembina on their own initiative, but there is persuasive evidence that while they were waiting for the governor's entourage to arrive, they were subjected to considerable lobbying by Stutsman and his confreres. Some time later a Yankton newspaper published a document, received from Pembina, which purported to contain a list of demands presented to McDougall by Kewetaosh and his followers as the price of entry to Rupert's Land.[27] McDougall made no reference to such a document in his detailed report of the meeting, and in a subsequent report he commented as follows on the newspaper story:

The letter was concocted by American schemers at Pembina, and read to the Indians who were waiting to see me. At first they consented to it, but the next day went to the village, asked to see it, and tore it up.[28]

The fact that the document showed up in the Yankton newspaper with which Stutsman maintained a regular correspondence about the insurrection indicates that the little lawyer probably played a part in this unsuccessful attempt to harness Indian fears. Three weeks later Stutsman was to take a copy of the letter to Winnipeg, where he explained the Indians' failure to present it to McDougall as follows:

... on hearing of the French Half-Breed movement in the settlement they drew back and did not present their letter fearing that if they did so it would be considered a joint Indian and Half-Breed movement and thereby hurt the cause of their Half-Breed brethren.[29]

Subsequent events were to demonstrate both the falsehood of this explanation and the extremely volatile nature of the forces with which Stutsman had attempted to meddle.

The letter to the Yankton paper was part of a very effective propaganda campaign that Stutsman and his Pembina friends waged against

McDougall over the next two months. The campaign had, in fact, begun even before the governor's arrival – with a letter written to the same Yankton newspaper the day after Stutsman's first interview with the Metis leaders in September.[30] While McDougall was conferring with the Indian delegation on November 1, Stutsman took up his pen again, this time to the St. Paul *Daily Press*, a journal he knew to have a large readership sympathetic to the annexationist cause, and to be scanned by major newspapers across the country.[31] It was the first of a stream of letters in which he and his colleagues provided readers in St. Paul and the nation at large with reasonably accurate but strongly biased accounts of the Red River insurrection. He also kept up a correspondence with Yankton and Sioux City newspapers, and occasionally with the other St. Paul journal, the *Pioneer*. Although Stutsman and most of the other participants in this propaganda war employed pseudonyms, most of his contributions can be identified fairly easily by internal clues. His letter of November 1 is notable for two reasons. First, it contained an early articulation of several of the principal demands that were to be included in the insurgents' first Bill of Rights, drawn up a month later.[32] Second, it displayed fore-knowledge of a pending event of which McDougall was blithely unaware as he sat talking to Chief Kewetaosh:

... before tomorrow morning an armed force will arrive at the Governor's quarters and compel him to recross the line into the United States.

The prediction was accurate. Upon learning that the governor-designate had entered the territory in defiance of its order, the Métis National Committee had dispatched an armed party, led by Ambroise Lépine, to demand his return to American soil. When the party dismounted on the evening of November 2 outside the stockade of the little trading post where McDougall was ensconced, they were met by Enos Stutsman, with whom they conferred briefly before going to speak to the governor.

In that first interview with Lépine, McDougall attempted to employ the same powers of persuasion with which he had managed to satisfy the Indians. If his account is to be believed, he was at least partially successful in convincing Lépine that he was already vested with legal authority over the territory by reason of his commission from the Queen, which he produced.[33] However, when Lépine and his men met again with Stutsman and others in Pembina later that evening, the lawyer must have explained that McDougall's commission could not take legal effect until after the transfer of jurisdiction from the Hudson's Bay Company to Canada. The Métis party was back at the trading post early the next morning, and resolutely escorted the governor and his entourage back across the border without even permitting them time for breakfast.[34] An eye-witness to the event, former Customs Collector Joseph Lemay, immediately wrote a colorful description of the ouster for the St. Paul *Daily Press*, reporting that "At this very time his future Excellency and party are preparing their breakfast in the timber growing on the banks of the majestical River of Pembina...."[35] A letter from Stutsman in the same issue of the *Daily Press* had a mocking tone that must have stung the self-important McDougall sharply:

A king without a kingdom is said to be poorer than a peasant. And I can assure you that a live Governor, with a full complement of officials, and menials from Attorney-General down to cooks and scullions, without one poor foot of territory, is a spectacle sufficiently sad to move the hardest heart.[36]

It was not just to newspapers that Stutsman directed his pen. Within hours of learning that McDougall was back in Pembina, he took it upon himself to write to the president of the United States:

Nov. 2, 1869

Sir

I should be deficient in my duty both as an official and as an American citizen if I did not solemnly call your attention to the situation as it exists in this part of the Continent of North America and the opportunity it offers for instant and decisive action on the part of the Government of the United States. At this moment this country is properly without any government, and a large number of its inhabitants – the majority, I believe – are favorably disposed to its annexation by the United States.[37]

If President Grant ever replied directly to Stutsman there is no known record of it. There can be little doubt, though, that the letter would have been brought to the attention of those in the Department of State who were monitoring Canadian and Rupert's Land affairs. They also received representatives that strongly opposed intervention. On November 22, the governor of Minnesota wrote to the president to say that J.W. Taylor, the government's consultant on the British colonies, would call on the president to present the governor's "solicitude that the National Government should carefully refrain from any interference that might possibly embroil the Indians on both sides of the International boundary and endanger the peace of our frontiers."[38] In the face of such conflicting advice, Grant decided to bide his time, and sent Taylor to Ottawa to observe events from that vantage point.

As Governor McDougall finished his belated breakfast beside the Pembina River after being escorted back across the border that bleak November morning, and began to ponder his next move, the seriousness of his position was disturbingly apparent. His first account of the expulsion concluded as follows: "There is a strong sympathy among the people here with the insurgents. We are not free from peril."[39] He was determined, however, to remain at Pembina until the situation improved, or he received instructions from Ottawa on how to deal with the predicament.

With winter fast approaching, McDougall's first concern was to arrange suitable accommodation for his party. Their tents were already uncomfortable, and the arrival of snow, which was expected any time, would render them entirely inadequate for people accustomed to the comforts of Toronto, Ottawa or Montreal. But as McDougall looked around him for available housing, the propects were not encouraging. "The village of Pembina," he reported to Ottawa: "consists of the house of the Postmaster, and another in which the Collector of Customs has his office. All the others, four or five in number, are mere huts, and offer... very poor accommodation for their present occupants."[40] When he attempted to rent such meagre housing as was available, he found that the inexorable laws of supply and demand, coupled with local sympathy for the rebels, had driven prices to extortionate levels. He indignantly rejected the offer of one small house at $500 for the winter,[41] and decided to look beyond the precincts of the village. Eventually he located a farmer named Larose, living about a mile south of Pembina, who was willing to rent his small, newly constructed cabin, and to build a temporary shanty to house his own family for the winter.[42] Larose's cabin proved to be too small for the governor's family and domestic retinue, however, so he ordered the construction of a somewhat larger building, which was not completed until after the snow began to fly. Even when complete, the governor's quarters were very primitive: essentially one sparsely furnished, drafty, room divided by canvas curtains. Lemay's snickering description of McDougall's cabin in the St. Paul *Daily Press* concluded with the observation that: "Three chairs and a small table are enough to furnish his frontier grot. A little of the frontier life hardships might soften his stiff neck."[43]

Other members of the entourage took accommodation where they could, in some cases with families that collaborated gleefully with Stutsman and the insurgents. A.N. Richards, who was McDougall's intended attorney general (and who was later to state that he never removed his clothes all the time he was in Pembina),[44] lodged with the Rolette family.[45] Stutsman was thus provided with a source of almost daily information about the fortunes of the beleaguered governor-designate.

This was by no means Stutsman's only source of information. He had eyes and ears throughout the village and district. Moreover, he lived with the postmaster, Charles Cavalier, who was an avowed annexationist. The temptation to examine postal communications to and from the governor would have been great, and there is evidence that the temptation was not resisted for long. Cavalier's refusal to cooperate in matters such as post office hours[46] and the acceptance of mail for the governor under cover to the postmaster[47] was a source of minor annoyance to McDougall almost from the beginning, and he soon became convinced that his mail was actually being tampered with:

The Post Office here is very loosely conducted, and is entirely at the service of the insurgents and their sympathizers. Many letters appear to have been opened, and the general opinion is that this *accident* occurs at Pembina. It might not be amiss if... (the Canadian Government)... requested the U.S. Postmaster General to instruct his subordinate here to show more care and courtesy in the conduct of his office than he has hitherto done.[48]

18. William McDougall's house near Pembina, D.T.

Partly because he did not trust the post office, and partly because he knew that mail pouches carried between Pembina and Fort Garry were being scrutinized by Métis guards at the St. Norbert barricade, McDougall found it necessary to use secret couriers to the British settlement. Among the first of these was a young military man, Major J. Wallace, who managed to pull the wool over even Stutsman's wary eyes for a while. Wallace had been travelling with the McDougall party, and had had a small falling-out with the governor before arriving at Pembina. News of the disagreement had reached the lawyer's alert ears, so when Wallace introduced himself to Stutsman it seemed plausible that he had severed his ties with McDougall. It turned out, moreover, that both men were members of the same secret society (presumably the Masonic Order), which made it all the easier to win Stutsman's confidence. The truth was that Wallace and McDougall had long since resolved their differences, and that Wallace was secretly working in the governor's interest. Stutsman had been empowered by Louis Riel to issue passes (short letters of introduction, actually) to strangers wishing to visit the British settlement. Wallace was able to obtain such a letter, and with it to gain easy access and egress to the settlement on McDougall's behalf.[49] He managed to keep his true allegiance secret for several weeks.[50]

Despite such minor victories, the awkwardness of McDougall's position was beginning to prey on his mind. Apart from the discomforts of his quarters, and the difficulty and expense of obtaining adequate provisions, his chief concerns were a lack of direction from Ottawa, and the uncooperative attitude of the Hudson's Bay Company's governor at Fort Garry. The latter officer was too ill to take decisive action. He was, moreover, of the opinion that McDougall's continued presence at Pembina was acting as a goad to the Métis community. These worries, aggravated by the taunts and sneers of local residents, had put the governor-designate in a very black mood. He began to exaggerate the dangers surrounding him. In a letter to the prime minister, November 8, he confided: "The situation is grave... I sleep with my revolver under my head and a good rifle near at hand."[51] Ten days later, he was in an even more desperate frame of mind:

19. Joseph Lemay

If they come to molest us on American soil we will *shoot* without hesitation, for this is the country where everyone shoots when he has a mind to, and the verdict when you shoot in self-defence always is "served 'em right." I don't think they will attempt it. I have exhibited my magazine guns and done some tall shooting myself, just to show their power, with Yankees and half-breeds standing about."[52]

McDougall was not the sort of man to sit back and wait for the enemy to come to him. As the aggressive tone of the last statement may indicate, he was formulating a plan of action, to be put into effect if he had still received no guidance from Ottawa by the end of the month.

In the meantime the attention of Pembina observers had shifted from the governor's predicament to exciting developments in the British settlement. Riel and the Métis National Committee had seized and occupied the Hudson's Bay Company fort at Fort Garry the same day McDougall was expelled. Then, seeking a mandate from a constituency broader than their own ethnic community, they had issued a proclamation calling for the election of representatives from every English-speaking parish in the area – a total of twelve representatives in all – to meet at the Fort Garry courthouse on November 16 with the twelve members of the Métis National Committee.

The invitation had thrown the English-speaking community into confusion. Apart from the Canadians, who were uniformly opposed to every action of the Métis, many English-speaking settlers were sympathetic to Riel's goals, although most deplored his methods. It was eventually decided, over the opposition of the Canadians, to choose the requested delegates, and to meet with the rebels. The first sessions of the conference were not successful, however. Riel was not well prepared, and he allowed himself to be drawn into a series of largely pointless debates about minor matters, rather than to search for areas of common agreement. It was perhaps fortunate that at this point the courthouse was needed for the regular session of the Quarterly Court of Assiniboia, and the conference adjourned for a few days. When it re-convened on November 23, Enos Stutsman was in Winnipeg.

Stutsman had arrived the previous day, bearing word portraits of the various members of the beseiged governor's party to entertain those with whom he shared stimulants at Emmerling's Hotel. McDougall he described as "overbearing, distant and unpleasant... vindictive towards the people of this country – and... heard to utter the threat that the French Half-Breeds would rue the day when they turned him out of Pembina Fort, and that he would see the time when he would have his foot on their necks."[53] Provencher and Richards were treated more kindly, though Stutsman suggested that the latter's knowledge of law was inadequate for someone who sought to be attorney general. Captain Cameron, whom Stutsman and his Pembina friends had taken to calling "the Penetrator" (in honor of Cameron's boast that he would soon lead a military force to "penetrate" the rebel territory)[54] and "Captain of the Horse Marines," was characterized as "a natural ass... no more fitted to be a member of the council than a real live donkey."[55] Cameron's wife, the daughter of a prominent Canadian politician, was described as "sprightly and pretty and altogether unfit[56] for such a mop as Captain Cameron."[57]

But Stutsman had not come to Winnipeg to entertain. In part he was there to observe; he was enabled by the visit to send the newspapers with which he was corresponding an accurate assessment of the points of view of the various segments of the local population. These he gleaned from informal discussions in such gathering places as Bannatyne and Begg's store.[58] His primary mission, however, seems to have been to advise and influence Riel and his supporters during their re-convoked discussions with the representatives of the English parishes. Alexander Begg, a moderate and reasonably objective observer of the unfolding scene, commented in his journal that:

The American residents in the Town of Winnipeg and those at Pembina have of late greatly interested themselves in the movements of the French and are evidently trying to mislead Riel in favor of annexation to the States. H.S. Donaldson, Major Robinson, Oscar Malmoras (sic), and Enos Stutsman at Pembina are all admitted to the secret councils of Riel.[59]

A few days late, Begg, who tried to remain on good terms with all parties, but confided his true feelings to his journal, recorded: "Two men arrived late in the night from Pembina with dispatches it is said for Col. Stutsman, who remains in the settlement – and it is feared that gentleman's influence here is not for the good of the people."[60]

Although the exact nature of Stutsman's contributions cannot be

20. Emmerling's Hotel, Winnipeg

known with certainty, it is probable that they were very influential. On November 24, after a day of petty rhetorical wrangles reminiscent of those on which the first session of the convention had been wasted, Riel suddenly changed the tone and direction of the debate. He proposed the formation of a provisional government, composed of equal numbers of French and English representatives, which could negotiate with Canada on behalf of the entire settlement, and could in the meantime provide interim government services. Riel's principal biographer suggests that the notion of establishing a provisional government may have been "whispered in his ear by Enos Stutsman."[61] He also points out other possible sources for the idea, but the Stutsman hypothesis is persuasive. Stutsman was, after all, an experienced parliamentarian (the only one on the scene), with a demonstrated knack for fashioning effective compromise solutions to legislative impasses. Both the boldness and the practicality of the proposal were Stutsman hallmarks. Furthermore, the lawyer's unquestionably key participation in the events of the next few days adds to the likelihood that he was also involved in the development of the provisional government scheme.

The idea took the English-speaking delegates to the convention so much by surprise that they called for an adjournment. For several days local discussions took place throughout the settlement in order to determine the response of the English parishes. When it began to appear that the establishment of a full provisional government was not favored, a compromise was suggested. The Hudson's Bay Company would continue to govern the territory internally, while the provisional regime negotiated with Canada. This compromise was advanced by moderates like Begg and Bannatyne, and supported by such American annexationists as United States Consul Oscar Malmros, Fenian leader W.B. O'Donoghue, and, probably, Enos Stutsman.[62] Riel would not accept so watered-down a version of the scheme about which he had become enthusiastic, however. When the convention re-assembled on December 1, hopes for a unified provisional government were at least temporarily dead.

Before the meeting dissolved, one further attempt was made to find a basis for English–French agreement, and Stutsman again appears to have played a key role. The date on which this final session of the convention was being held, December 1, was significant. It had been announced by the Canadian government as the probable date of the transfer of legal jurisdiction over Rupert's Land to Canadian control. Several of the English-speaking delegates to the convention raised this as a reason for ceasing all further resistance to McDougall's entry. Riel's response to this line of argument was conciliatory:

If Mr. McDougall is really our Governor today, our chances are better than ever. He has no more to do than prove to us his desire to treat us well. If he guarantees our rights, I am one of those who will go to meet him in order to escort him as far as the seat of his government.[63]

He was immediately challenged to produce a list of the guarantees in return for which he would consent to the governor's entry, and he requested a short adjournment for that purpose.

Although Riel's leading biographer claims that he did not have a list of rights prepared at that point, he was able to produce one when the meeting re-convened two hours later.[64] How had he been able to respond so rapidly to an apparently unexpected demand? One answer is that he and his colleagues had been discussing their grievances for months, and were in general agreement as to what they wanted. That does not, however, explain the speed with which the thirteen demands were articulated in precise and reasonably graceful English. The explanation appears to be that Enos Stutsman had come to Riel's rescue. Among Riel's list of thirteen guarantees, the five that Stutsman had communicated to the St. Paul *Daily Press* a full month previously all appeared prominently, four of them among the first six listed. Even the language was little changed.[65] Some items had a distinctly American flavor, such as, "The Legislature to have the power to pass all laws local to the Territory, over the veto of the Executive, by a two-third vote."[66] The inference that Stutsman was called in to assist Riel in the preparation of the list is difficult to resist.

The first twelve points in Riel's list were items upon which most of the delegates, both English and French, agreed. But the final point, and for Riel the essential one, was impossible for the English to accept: that McDougall would not be admitted to the territory until he either guaranteed the listed rights personally or procured an act of the Canadian Parliament doing so.[67] Unable to find any acceptable common ground on this issue, the convention collapsed, with Riel angrily informing the English delegates that the Métis intended to proceed unilaterally.[68]

Stutsman returned to Pembina a day or two after the convention dissolved. Whether this was merely because his tactical and legal advice was no longer required, or, as McDougall was to suggest, because of fear for his personal safety, is a matter for conjecture. McDougall had finally launched the attack he had been planning, and Enos Stutsman was one of its initial targets.

Although he had not yet received confirmation that the transfer of legal jurisdiction to Canada would indeed take place on December 1 as scheduled, McDougall had decided to gamble that it would. Relying on the legal authority that the transfer would give him, he prepared to take military measures against the rebel regime. First he drafted a proclamation in the Queen's name, dated December 1, announcing that the settlement was Canadian territory, and that all governmental authority was vested in him as lieutenant governor. He then arranged for Colonel J.S. Dennis, the chief of the ill-fated survey operation, to have the document printed on the press of the pro-Canadian *Nor'Wester*, and distributed throughout the settlement on proclamation day. At the same time, he issued a commission to Colonel Dennis, appointing him "lieutenant and conservator of the peace" as of the date of the proclamation, with the power to "raise, organize, arm, equip and provision a sufficient force... to attack, arrest, disarm or disperse the... armed men so unlawfully assembled and disturbing the public peace; and for that purpose... to assault, fire upon, pull down or break into any fort, house, stronghold, or other place in which the said armed men may be found."[69]

On the evening of December 1, under cover of darkness and a snowstorm, McDougall proceeded to Canadian territory to read his proclamation and, as he thought, to legitimize the drastic measures he had put in motion. Stutsman's report of the event for the St. Paul *Daily Press*, while based on hearsay and embroidered by the writer's cruel wit, is worth quoted at length, if only to demonstrate his way with words:

On the 1st instant, at the hour of 10 p.m., while the mercury indicated 20° below zero, and Old Boreas was on a bender, seven lonely pedestrians, fully armed and equipped, might have been (and were) seen stemming the blast, and, as best they could, shaping their course in the direction of the oak post marking the international boundary – their brows contracted with firm resolve to do or die.

This intrepid little band consisted of Governor McDougall and his entire official staff.

His Excellency was armed with the Queen's proclamation, the Dominion flag, and two pointer dogs. The fat Attorney-General felt quite secure with an old-fashioned Colt, that had not been discharged for fifteen years, while the Collector of Customs (of a more practical turn of mind), thinking that the aforesaid Boreas would prove the most formidable enemy he should encounter very wisely armed himself with a well charged flask of "forty rod" – hence, while the other members of the party were shivering like frightened puppies – the festive Collector felt as comfortable as could be expected.

On nearing the boundary a skirmish line was advanced – to reconnoiter – and finding all save the firmament, clear, a charge was sounded, and, on double-quick, the brave little band dashed across the line into much coveted territory; whereupon the Dominion flag was unfurled, and, in defiance of the blinding storm and the inky darkness, Mr. McDougall, in the name of that government, assumed formal possession of the great Northwest Territory. After which the entire command, elated with victory, returned in triumph to their quarters on Uncle Sam's side of the international boundary.

And *thus* was accomplished the conquest of the Northwest Territory.[70]

It is easy to understand why this brilliant little man, whom McDougall had begun to refer to as the "prime conspirator,"[71] so infuriated the governor and his party, and why Colonel Dennis, in his capacity as "conservator of the peace," intended to move against Stutsman before anyone else. Ironically, the lawyer seems to have been saved by his adversary in the McLean trial, Judge John Black. On December 2, the day after the convention had dissolved and McDougall's proclamation had been distributed, Dennis reported to the Governor that he had employed some Indian mercenaries. He continued:

I sent Judge Black a request last evening that he would call upon me, and he has accordingly been here a good part of the day. I wished to consult him as to the expediency of my proclaiming Martial Law in the Territory, so as to enable me to seize upon Stuttsman (sic), who still remains at Winnipeg, no doubt aiding and abetting the Rioters. The idea of such a thing seemed to frighten him, and he begged of me to delay it a day or two... Should we succeed in getting hold of the prime conspirator named, I shall put him in a strong room in this place, under the charge of my friend Prince, the Indian Chief and his warriors, until he may be delivered by some due, but, we shall hope, tedious course of law.[72]

It does not accord with Stutsman's feisty nature that he would have hastened his departure from Winnipeg in order to evade arrest or avoid the pending hostilities, as McDougall claimed when the lawyer returned to Pembina.[73] It is more likely that he simply regarded his work in the settlement as complete for the time being. In any event, his spirited description of the governor's border foray puts the lie to McDougall's added comment that Stutsman was "very subdued and crestfallen" when he arrived home.[74]

If anyone had reason to be crestfallen, it would soon be McDougall himself. Colonel Dennis's mission was not going well. More important than his failure to gain the judge's support for a declaration of martial law were the disappointing results of his recruiting campaign. Other than his Indian mercenaries, who were camped near his headquarters at Lower Fort Garry (the "stone fort"), some twenty miles north of Winnipeg, and about fifty Canadians who had rallied enthusiastically to arms and had gathered at John Schultz's Winnipeg home, Dennis's army was meagre. The bulk of the English-speaking population, whose refusal to participate in Riel's proposed provisional government he had construed as a token of willingness to resist the rebels, turned out to be opposed to any armed confrontation, even at the instance of constituted authority. Dennis decided to delay any aggressive steps against the insurgents until his force was a little stronger.[75]

Riel then moved rapidly to ensure that this would never happen. He strengthened his garrison, commandeered all firearms in local shops, and closed down the Canadians' propaganda organ, the *Nor'Wester*. Then, on December 7, Riel's men surrounded and captured without violence the armed contingent assembled at John Schultz's house. At the same time a force was sent to occupy the Hudson's Bay Company post at North Pembina, which was McDougall's chief source of food and other supplies. On December 8, Riel issued a "Declaration of the People of Rupert's Land and the Northwest," proclaiming, among other things, that "a People, when it has no Government, is free to adopt one form of government in preference to another, to give or to refuse allegiance to that which is proposed." He announced the establishment of a provisional government. The provisional government was stated to be headed by Riel, and to have existed since November 24, when Riel had first broached the idea to the convention of French and English representatives.

It is sometimes alleged that this document, like the earlier list of rights, was the work of Enos Stutsman.[76] This is unlikely. It is true that Stutsman announced it to the world in a letter to the St. Paul *Daily Press* on December 13.[77] It is also true that the statement had a somewhat American tone, and that it was referred to from the beginning as Riel's Declaration of Independence. It does not exhibit Stutsman's writing style, however, and it appears to have been prepared after he returned to Pembina. A leading historian contends that "the argument and the idiom of the document are Riel's... ," though the final composition was probably the work of a priest who was close to the rebels.[78] The Americanisms were probably contributed by the American Fenian, W.B. O'Donoghue, who had by this time become one of Riel's chief lieutenants. It was O'Donoghue's influence that caused the new flag of the provisional government, when it was raised over Fort Garry on December 10, to display a shamrock together with the fleur-de-lis.[79]

Dennis's employment of Indians had been an egregious tactical error. Although McDougall had cautioned him against engaging substantial numbers of Indians for the time being,[80] the governor's reports make it clear that he actively participated in the efforts to win the support of the natives. On December 2, for example, he exulted that Chief Peguis had offered the services of his Cree warriors to help put down the rebellion, and he acknowledged his role in causing the offer to be made:

I have taken pains, through the agency of loyal persons having influence with them, to arouse the apprehensions of the Indians in reference to the annexation features of the half-breed movement, and its effect upon them and their land claims. They have been quick to perceive that the outbreak bodes no good for them.... "[81]

Stutsman and his colleagues made devastating propaganda use of these ill-considered initiatives. In his first letter to the St. Paul *Daily Press* after returning from Winnipeg, Stutsman reported that Dennis had employed an Indian force, and that the use of such a force had been "openly justified" by Attorney General-Designate Richards in a conversation with Stutsman and other Pembina residents. Then, after grossly misrepresenting his own earlier effort to mobilize the Indians against McDougall as a spontaneous protest which had been withdrawn "through the influence of the present heads of the provisional government," he commented piously:

... however incredible it may appear, it is nevertheless true, that Mr. McDougall is willing to enlist even the savage in order to force his yoke upon a Christian people...

I trust that the people of Minnesota, who have had a sad experience of Sioux atrocities, will at once call the attention of our military authorities to our defenceless condition.[82]

News that Indians were to be employed in the hostilities outraged the other residents of Pembina. Even N.E. Nelson, the new United States deputy collector of customs, who had been one of the few American officials to adopt an ojective and courteous posture to the stranded governor, became livid with anger after being told of the conversation in which Attorney General Richards justified the use of Indians. When McDougall learned of Nelson's reaction he realized that something had to be done to calm Pembina opinion. The governor-designate proceeded hastily to the village and called on Nelson, requesting a meeting with him and other community leaders. The meeting was quickly assembled. Stutsman was not present, perhaps at McDougall's request, or perhaps because he refused to be summoned by a foreign official. Several of his cronies were there, however: Charles Cavalier and both Joe Rolettes, father and son. Also prominent at the meeting was former Customs Collector Joseph Lemay, who still recalled vividly having to flee from Pembina to Fort Garry the last time the Indians were on the warpath. The discussion, which both McDougall and Lemay recorded in great detail,[83] did not do much to shift public opinion. Although he denied having authorized the use of Indians, and subsequently gave Nelson a letter addressed to Dennis instructing the latter not to do so, McDougall's tone was arrogant. He couldn't resist stating that if Indian war did break out it would serve right the persons who had attempted to instigate the Indians against *him* a month previously. He left the meeting with Joseph Lemay's ominous words ringing in his ears: "Let me tell you, sir, if you don't use your influence to keep the Indians out of this movement your life is not worth five cents."[84]

Following this tense scene, the members of McDougall's party who had been billeted in the village withdrew to his small cabin on the Larose farm, where: "... we established a military *regime*, and prepared to resist an attack from any quarter. We kept watch by day and by night, and had all our arms ready for action."[85] That he had not learned much from the episode, and did not yet appreciate how his tactics served the annexationist interest, are evident from some of the observations contained in his report to Ottawa:

The friendly disposition of the Indians of this Territory to us, and their antipathy to the Americans, is the great anchor by which we shall be enabled to hold it...

In these circumstances it was felt to be a wise as well as a loyal and humane policy to *threaten* the insurgents and their annexation leaders with an Indian as well as a civil war, if they persisted in their rebellious designs... I believe they have called for troops from the nearest American Post (Fort Abercrombie) to protect them from the dreaded Sioux.[86]

Whether Enos Stutsman ever had any genuine fear of an Indian uprising as a result of McDougall's or Dennis's efforts may be doubted. Some historians have suggested that his primary motivation was to create a situation, or the appearance of a situation, that would convince the American authorities to send troops to the Pembina area.[87] It will be remembered that he had been calling for a local garrison for a long time. The presence of United States troops would facilitate any annexation move that Washington might decide upon, and it would certainly have a beneficial effect on land values in the Pembina area. Whatever may have been going on in Stutsman's complex mind, however, his letters to the editor and those of his Pembina and Winnipeg allies kindled real fear in the hearts of many people on both sides of the border who had previously experienced the terrors of Indian warfare. It did not take long before the newspapers were clogged with often fanciful accounts of apprehended Indian attacks, and eloquent pleas for military assistance. If McDougall had set out to smooth the way for an American snatch of Rupert's Land, he could hardly have done a more effective job.

By now, Colonel Dennis knew that the game was up. Schultz and his Canadians were in prison, the double agent Wallace had been discovered,[88] the recruiting campaign had gone sour, and Dennis was being criticized for employing Indians. In desperation, he attempted to save face by issuing a proclamation stating that in view of Riel's public declaration Dennis accepted the rebels' desire for peace and willingness to negotiate. Therefore, the proclamation continued:

I now call on and order the loyal party in the Northwest Territories to cease further action under the appeal to arms made by me; and I call on the French party to satisfy the people of their sincerity in wishing for a peaceful ending of all these troubles by sending a deputation to the Lieutenant-Governor at Pembina without unnecessary delay.[89]

To what extent this move salvaged Dennis's dignity in the eyes of settlers who knew that most of the "loyal party" were now languishing in the cells of Fort Garry is open to speculation. After paying off his Indian mercenaries, Dennis left the stone fort for Pembina disguised, if letters to the editor are to be credited, as an Indian woman.[90]

The final blow came when McDougall learned, on eventually receiving directions from Ottawa, that the transfer of legal authority had not taken place on December 1 as he had assumed. The Canadian Government had decided at the last moment, because of the unsettled situation in Rupert's Land, to delay the formal transfer. Not only had Dennis's ineffectual "counter-revolution" been illegal, therefore, but McDougall's proclamation, which had caused the local Hudson's Bay Company authorities to relinquish their governmental responsibilities, had confirmed the assertion in Riel's declaration that there was "no Government." This provided a patina of legality for the provisional government. Even Prime Minister Macdonald acknowledged that: "In such a case... it is quite open by the law of nations for the inhabitants to form a Government *ex necessitate*, for the protection of life and property... "[91]

McDougall now had no alternative but to withdraw. On December 17, after one last futile attempt to communicate with Riel,[92] he packed his belongings and most of his entourage into the sleighs he had been constructing to carry them to Fort Garry, and headed south instead – toward Fort Abercrombie and thence to the head of the railway line at St. Cloud. As they took their leave, would-be Attorney General Richards bitterly warned a grinning Enos Stutsman that he and his friends would "have cause to regret" their support of the rebel cause.[93] The threat would be put to good use in Stutsman's continuing propaganda campaign to convince American authorities that an Indian war was looming.

When his party reached St. Paul, McDougall gave long interviews to reporters of both city newspapers, in which he laid the primary blame for the Red River insurrection at the feet of Enos Stutsman:

From first to last, Col. Stutsman, claiming to be an American, has been the head and front of the rebellion. He is Riel's adviser and plans every move that Riel makes. It was Stutsman who counselled the Governor's capture and the seizing of Fort Garry. It was Stutsman who wrote the declaration of independence which was issued, and who vises every document that is put forward in Bruce's or Riel's name, and it was Stutsman who set on foot the many glaring falsehoods calculated to arouse and inflame the passions of the French half-breeds engaged in the rebellion.[94]

This was a grotesquely distorted view of Stutsman's role; McDougall had allowed his judgment to be warped by Stutsman's infuriating omnipresence. McDougall was prone to that sort of distortion; he was letter to claim in print that Joseph Howe, the Canadian cabinet minister to whom he had been responsible, and who was severely critical of McDougall's actions, had been "the chief abettor, if not the chief instigator, of the 'Red River Insurrection'."[95] While it may have been true that Howe's failure to keep the governor-designate adequately informed had been largely responsible for the fiasco, McDougall's exaggeration lost him the support of those who might otherwise have been sympathetic.

As December drew to a close, Enos Stutsman must have appeared, even to the most objective observers, to occupy center stage in the Red River drama. McDougall had left the scene after having torn a gaping hole in the governmental fabric of the territory. Riel's provisional government was in firm *de facto* (and arguably lawful) control. The Fenian O'Donoghue shared power with Riel, and the rest of the local annexationists, apparently led by Enos Stutsman, seemed to have Riel's complete confidence. The movement for United States military intervention to suppress apprehended Indian warfare, which Stutsman had instigated, now had a momentum of its own. Stutsman's newspaper correspondence included Washington journals.[96] Senator Ramsey had recently caused the United States Senate to pass a resolution requesting the president to report to the senate all information available about the Red River situation.[97] And rumors were circulating that Stutsman would soon be returning to Winnipeg, perhaps for good. The ever-observant Alexander Begg recorded in his journal for December 20, 1869, that "H.M. Robinson assisted by Col. Stutsman who is coming to reside among us is about starting a newspaper in the interests of the French."[98]

As a member of the Dakota Territorial Council, Stutsman should have been in Yankton by then, but the drama that was unfolding on his doorstep was too exciting (and potentially rewarding) to miss, so he had chosen to absent himself for at least the 1869-70 session. For the time being he intended to devote his entire energies to keeping north-central North America out of the clutches of what he called "that puffy little Dominion."[99] At the age of forty-three he was in the midst of the greatest adventure of his life.

Besides the opportunities for real estate speculation, which were never far from Stutsman's mind, an American-owned or independent Rupert's Land offered great political promise for those who played important roles in the "war of independence." What better tool with which to reap both commercial and political advantage than the community's newspaper? Stutsman had long since displayed a keen awareness of the power of the press, as well as a masterly ability to manipulate it. There had been no newspaper in the settlement since Riel closed down the *Nor'Wester*. When Stutsman returned to Pembina from Winnipeg in early December, he had been accompanied by Henry Robinson, a prominent American resident in Winnipeg,[100] with whom he discussed the possibility of a journalistic partnership. There is some evidence that they may have tried unsuccessfully to recruit as their partner or editor James Ross, an experienced journalist who had once edited the *Nor'Wester* and had lost a Hudson's Bay Company appointment because of his strongly anti-Company editorials.[101] The idleness of the *Nor'Wester* equipment presented a golden opportunity to acquire a ready-made printing plant at what would likely be a bargain price. And Louis Riel, it seemed, was benevolently disposed to both the proposed new journal and its American proprietors.

Stutsman did not go to Winnipeg immediately. This may have been because he was starting to take his own stories of impending Indian violence seriously, or because he had a lot of correspondence to complete, or perhaps even because he looked forward to spending a festive season at home with the Cavaliers for the first time in years. The most likely reason, however, is that he wanted a chance to assess the various emissaries he knew to be on their way to Rupert's Land from Canada, and who would likely pause at Pembina before continuing on to Fort Garry.

First came the team of the Very Reverend J.B. Thibault, a highly respected prairie missionary, and Colonel Charles de Salaberry, a French-Canadian soldier of sympathetic mien. Their mission was to convince the insurgents of Canada's good faith. Leaving de Salaberry in Pembina temporarily, Father Thibault went on alone, arriving at St. Norbert late on Christmas Day. Stutsman attempted to prejudice his reception by the insurgents with a letter to Riel:

Dear General,

I wish you and your friends a very happy Christmas...

If it be deemed necessary to confer with the Canadian Commissioners, would it not be advisable that such conference should take place on this frontier? I am afraid that if de Salaberry and Father Thibault (who I see by recent Canadian papers is just as much of a commissioner as Col. de Salaberry) are permitted to have free communication with your people they will give you trouble. Inasmuch as Father Thibault comes in an official capacity he should be regarded as an official and *not* as a minister of Christ. If he *being an official agent of the Canadian Government* be admitted – why reject McDougall or de Salaberry?

Regards to friend Donoghue.[102]

This letter seems to have done Stutsman's cause more harm than good. It was intercepted and copied by some of the settlement's moderates, including Alexander Begg,[103] whom it seems to have alarmed. If the original was permitted to reach Riel, which is not known, it may well have been thought to cast aspersions on a kindly and well-loved priest who, after a short time in the settlement, was won over to the rebel's point of view, anyway. Moreover, since neither Thibault nor de Salaberry had any authority to negotiate on behalf of the Canadian Government, and neither was skilled in the art of politics, there was never any real danger that they would undermine the insurrection.

Stutsman's letter to Riel also mentioned another Canadian who had shown up in Pembina on Christmas Eve: Dr. Charles Tupper from Nova Scotia. Physician turned politician, Tupper was one of Canada's "fathers of confederation," and was destined to become prime minister. At this time he was a very influential member of the Dominion Parliament. Tupper's mission was primarily personal.[104] He was the father of Captain Cameron's wife, and when he heard stories about possible Indian hostilities in the Red River Valley, he decided to travel to the area and bring his daughter home. Apparently he didn't think much more of his son-in-law's capabilities than Stutsman did. As it happened, the Camerons had not travelled south with McDougall, and when Tupper arrived he found them living in the ex-governor-designate's log cabin. The reason they had not yet left was that most of their personal possessions were being held at Fort Garry. Cameron had made his famous tilt at the St. Norbert barricade with his wife and two tons of furniture and other belongings in tow. When the Camerons were escorted back to the border their property was taken to Fort Garry and locked up there. The captain and his wife were understandably reluctant to return to Canada without their possessions, but since he was decidedly *persona non grata* north of the border the prospects for recovering them seemed bleak. Dr. Tupper undertook to travel to Fort Garry and seek the release of the property. It would, incidentally, give him an opportunity for some informal contact with the rebel leaders. The prime minister had asked him to make the attempt.

On the day after Christmas Dr. Tupper asked Joe Rolette Jr. to take him to Fort Garry. Rolette replied that he would do so if Colonel Stutsman would issue Tupper a pass. But when Rolette approached Stutsman, the lawyer warily told him to inform Tupper that he had no power to grant such passes, and that even if he had the authority he would not compromise the American Government by doing so. Enos Stutsman was not going to provide the Canadian Government easy evidence of international intrigue!

Tupper was also a canny politican – and a stubborn one. He had, as it happened, been called to the Cavalier home on Christmas day, to treat one of the postmaster's daughters for a sudden illness. He now returned to the home, ostensibly to give further instructions for the girl's treatment, but actually to speak to Stutsman. Charming as always, Stutsman apologized for being unable to assist Tupper. In view of the doctor's kindness to the Cavalier family, he said, he would like to help, but was powerless to do so. Tupper asked if he could at least suggest who to contact for permission to enter the settlement. Backed into a corner, Stutsman reluctantly advised him to see Father Ritchot at St. Norbert.

This was precisely what the wiley Canadian was seeking: an introduction, of sorts, to the man he knew was probably Riel's most influential adviser. He persuaded one of old Joe Rolette's younger sons to drive him, and set off for St. Norbert in a horse-drawn dog sled. After a series of misadventures, Tupper eventually met Riel, and arranged to have the Camerons' property returned. Although he did not discuss the uprising with Riel, he did so at length with Father Ritchot.

Dr. Tupper's conversations with the enigmatic priest do not appear to have had any effect on subsequent developments. There is a possibility, however, that the course of events was influenced by a chance encounter between Tupper and former Customs Collector Joseph Lemay.

Lemay had been an even more tireless writer of letters to the editor than Stutsman. Most issues of the St. Paul *Daily Press* carried side-by-side accounts of the rebellion by "Spectator" (Stutsman) and "Liberty" (Lemay). The former were more witty and often more accurate; the latter were longer and more detailed. Like Stutsman, Lemay had Riel's ear. In fact, at this moment Lemay may have been a good deal closer to the Métis leader than was the lawyer.

When Tupper first met Riel at Fort Garry, he found the rebel leader closeted with two men: Father Ritchot and Joseph Lemay. And when Tupper stayed overnight at Ritchot's house in St. Norbert, Riel and Lemay were also present. While at Ritchot's, Lemay received word from Pembina that his daughter had fallen ill with the same complaint as Cavalier's daughter. He decided to rush home in the company of Dr. Tupper. Tupper claimed to have converted Lemay to his views about the insurrection during the long sleigh-ride back to Pembina.[105] It is certainly true that Lemay became a strong opponent of annexation, and that he made himself unpopular in some quarters by the strength of his arguments in favor of negotiating with Canada. It is improbable that he underwent a sudden conversion during the journey with Dr. Tupper, however. One thing that had distinguished Lemay's letters from Stutsman's all along was the absence of annexationist sentiments. Whether stemming from deep-seated belief, from rejection of a political system that had hurt him, or from simple resentment of Stutsman, Joseph Lemay's opposition to United States annexation of Rupert's Land was his own. It is probable, however, that this attitude was strengthened by his conversations with Charles Tupper during the long sled ride back to Pembina. Given the views he held about both annexation and Stutsman, Lemay's close rapport with Louis Riel did not bode well for the Pembina lawyer.

The final ambassador from the Canadian Government to Louis Riel – and the most important – was Donald A. Smith, a Hudson's Bay Company official with a special and partly secret mandate from the prime minister. Smith had travelled as far as Pembina with Dr. Tupper, but had established his initial base of operations at the Hudson's Bay Company post at North Pembina rather than in the village. This enabled him to escape Stutsman's intelligence network. It was a token of the astuteness that would enable Smith to exert a profound influence on the course of subsequent events.

Smith arrived in the British settlement in early January, a few days after Tupper had left. Stutsman remained at Pembina, perhaps awaiting word of the effect of the Thibault, de Salaberry, Tupper and Smith missions; but his arrival in Winnipeg was expected daily.

The delay may have been related to confusion that seems to have arisen concerning the proprietorship of the proposed new newspaper. Begg's journal for December 22 stated that the owner of the printing equipment had agreed to sell it to Robinson and Stutsman, and that the latter would be on the scene soon.[106] It also claimed that the paper would espouse "the interests of the French." Two days later there was a rumor among the French-speaking population that one of their own number had bought the equipment.[107] Begg noted on December 26 that Stutsman had not yet arrived (adding cynically, "but is working for *his* cause where he is").[108] The next day, Begg recorded that the deal had not yet been closed. The French resident who was earlier said to have bought the equipment was reported to be lending most of the purchase price to Robinson on the understanding that the paper would be conducted "in the interests of the people." Robinson had denied this, and had asserted that "it is purely a private enterprise between him and Stutsman."[109] Then, on December 28, Joseph Lemay suddenly entered the scene:

Mr. LeMay (sic) late collector of Customs at Pembina was in town to-day. It appears that he has been anticipating taking part in the conducting of the new newspaper to be started in the interests of the French party. On being told that Stutsman was calculating to belong to the paper or part of the paper to belong to him LeMay (sic) seemed put out and stated that the information he had received might change his plans, and instead of starting at once for Pembina as he intended it would necessitate a visit to St. Boniface. Stutsman and LeMay (sic) are on bad terms with each other and it is evident that it has been kept a secret from him Stutsman's proposed connection with the paper. Has Stutsman backed out or what? The bargain between Coldwell and Robinson for the printing press was completed today and the money paid over...[110]

This, it should be noted, was the day Tupper first saw Lemay conferring with Riel. The next day, December 29, as Tupper and Lemay were hurrying back to Pembina, Begg reported that "... Jos. LeMay (sic)... is to have nothing to do with the coming newspaper."[111]

What had happened? The hypothesis that Stutsman had schemed to keep his involvement in the project secret from Lemay in order to obtain the latter's participation does not stand up in light of their differing views about annexation. Perhaps someone in the French community (Father Ritchot?) had attempted to keep Stutsman out of the project by locating an alternative source of funding, and by proposing Lemay as a participant, but had been unsuccessful in persuading Robinson to adopt the new arrangement. Robinson succeeded in launching the newspaper January 7, 1870, presumably with only Stutsman's financial support. The frustration of Lemay's journalistic ambitions by his Pembina rival no doubt strengthened the conviction with which he concurred in Tupper's condemnation of Stutsman's annexation schemes.

The first issue of the fledgling newspaper, called the *New Nation*, adopted a frankly annexationist stance, though it supported interim independence as a step toward annexation.[112] By this time American Consul Oscar Malmros was also working quite openly to persuade the insurgents to move in that direction. A few days after the paper appeared, Begg commented:

The American Consul has been trying to get Riel to take in Major Robinson as Secretary and H.S. Donaldson as Adjutant – but so far without success – a pretty kettle of fish indeed. It only needs Stutsman as Comptroller of the Revenue Department and Cavalier Postmaster General to make the thing complete – eh bien! We will see what we will see.[113]

The efforts of the Americans seemed to be approaching a climax. Several prominent residents of Pembina – Joe Rolette Jr., N.E. Nelson, Joseph Lemay – had either arrived in Winnipeg or were on their way.[114] On the evening of January 10, Enos Stutsman finally made his appearance at Emmerling's Hotel. Two days later, an American flag was seen flying (at half-mast) from the hotel's staff, and although

Oscar Malmros, who lived in the hotel, explained it as a mere gesture of mourning for the recent death of the United States Secretary of War,[115] most lookers-on regarded it as the battle standard of Winnipeg's annexationists.[116]

The standard-bearer, it seemed, would be Colonel Enos Stutsman. He was, by this time, receiving considerable attention from the American press, primarily as a result of McDougall's widely re-printed accusations. The *Sioux City Daily Times* told its readers that Stutsman was the "secretary of the settlers who now propose to throw off the British yoke," and remarked that he was "on the right road to fame and success."[117] The Yankton *Union and Dakotian* called him "the brains of the Red River Rebellion," described him as "in every... respect the beau ideal of a gallant and accomplished gentleman," and observed that his "numerous friends will be glad to hear of his influence in behalf of Freedom."[118] The St. Paul *Pioneer*, which opposed Stutsman politically, offered its readers a more balanced assessment, characterizing him as one who:

... has been a warm friend and a bitter enemy to the same men in the same year. He is a sharp and scheming Yankee; smooth and captivating in conversation; genteel and temperate in habits; daring in deeds; ambitious of fame, and susceptible of mischief... He is just the man to plan, impel and guide a border rebellion among so excitable and impulsive a populace as the half-breed French... in activity, pluck and acuteness he stands head and shoulders with the shrewdest of men.[119]

James Wickes Taylor, who was still monitoring the Red River situation for the secretary of state, reported Stutsman's arrival in Winnipeg to the secretary of state with the comment that he was: "a person of sagacity, cultivation and great force of character."[120]

Alexander Begg did not look upon Stutsman's arrival favorably. In recording that the colonel had "brought his traps intending to remain in the Settlement for a month or two," Begg commented sourly, "Stutsman is up to something and it is to be hoped he will get sold."[121] There were other ill omens as well. A few days previously, for example, Begg had described the fate of Stutsman's letter to Riel about Thibault:

The letter... was found the other day inside the Fort – lying on the ground with the signature torn off. It seemed as if it had been used in the performance of a natural duty in which man must necessarily place one hand behind him – directing it towards the end of his spine – enough said![122]

More significantly, Riel had reacted angrily to the annexationist tone of the *New Nation's* first issue, and had reprimanded editor Robinson about it.[123] As the unexpected antipathy stirred up among the French-speaking population by the sight of Old Glory fluttering over the Emmerling Hotel was to show, [124] local enthusiasm for union with the United States had been grossly overestimated. And when Stutsman propelled himself into Emmerling's that night and called for a warming beverage he was concerned to learn that he had been proceded earlier in the day by the principal French anti-annexationist, Joseph Lemay.[125]

The next morning, Stutsman hastened to Fort Garry to confer with Riel, but he missed him. He had to be content with leaving a note:

My dear General:

I called this morning to see you on some very important business, but you was (sic) just starting away with a party and I concluded not to detain you.

Will you my esteemed friend drop me a line to inform me at what hour tomorrow it will suit your convenience to meet me (in *strictly* private conversation) at my room at the Emmerling House.

As I desire to see you *alone* I think it best to meet in my room where we will not be interrupted.

I must start for Pembina Thursday morning, and therefore must see you tomorrow if at all.[126]

The reference to having to return to Pembina is interesting in view of Begg's observation that Stutsman had brought enough gear to stay for a month or two. It may have been just a ploy to ensure an early appointment with Riel, but even that explanation indicates an awareness that the rebel leader did not regard his arrival in the settlement as an event of great import. Stutsman's senstive eyes and ears

Winnipeg, Jan 11. 1870

My dear General —

I called this morning to see you on some very important business, but you was just starting away with a party and I concluded not to detain you. —

Will you my esteemed friend drop me a line to inform me at what hour tomorow it will suit your convenience to meet me (in strictly private conversation) at my room at the Emmerling House. —

As I desire to see you alone I think it best to meet in my room where we will not be interrupted. —

I must start for Pembina thursday morning & therefore must see you to morow if at al. —

Believe me dear General to be
As ever
Your friend &
Obt servant
E. Stutsman.

21. Letter from Stutsman to Riel, January 11, 1870

had probably already picked up enough clues to realize what most of his American cronies did not yet understand – that the insurgents were not ready to consider United States annexation seriously.

It is not known what transpired at Stutsman's meeting with Riel if, indeed, it ever took place. While it is likely that they did meet, it is certain that Riel gave the American no firmer commitment than to consider the desirability of union with the United States *if* negotiations with Canada should turn out to be impossible or unproductive. On January 13, the day after the requested meeting, Alexander Begg made the following entry in his journal with obvious relish:

Col. Stutsman begins to find his game about played out in the settlement and instead of remaining a month or two as he intended he has made up his mind to leave for Pembina tomorrow. Poor Americans they have played their hand openly and not too well.[127]

The following day he recorded: "Col. Stutsman left today for Pembina disgusted!!!"[128] And on January 26: "The American flag was lowered and taken down today."[129]

Why had Stutsman's mission failed? In part, perhaps, because Lemay had been undermining Riel's confidence in Stutsman. Fundamentally, however, the failure was the result of a serious misreading of local opinion. Loyalty to the British connection remained strong among the vast majority of Rupert's Land residents, French, English and Indian. While the status of an independent Crown colony might have been preferred by most at that point to a union with Canada, the extremely influential Roman Catholic clergy and lay leaders, like Joseph Lemay, favored negotiations with Canada. Donald Smith's manipulations, together with Riel's continuing desire to unite the English and French elements of the community, were pushing the insurgents in the same direction. It strengthened the rebels' bargaining position, of course, to appear interested in United States annexation, and Riel skilfully preserved that appearance as long as he could. This probably explains the retention of the Fenian W.B. O'Donoghue in a position of great apparent power and influence even after his personal relations with Riel were strained. By the time Stutsman came to see him in January, Riel had no real intention of pursuing the American solution, except as a bargaining club or, perhaps, as a last resort.

Uncharacteristically, Enos Stutsman had been taken in by Riel's game. Now he knew better. As he shielded his face from the searing January winds on the sixty-mile journey home, he must have realized that the only possibility of annexation lay in the failure of Donald Smith's mission to promote negotiations between Canada and the rebellious settlement, or of the ensuing negotiations themselves. The knowledge that he and his colleagues had become mere tools of the sagacious (or well-advised) young rebel leader does not seem to have embittered him. He was, after all, a calloused professional in the no-holds-barred game of politics. Besides, he knew that annexation was still a distinct, if now remote, possibility, and he would not burn any bridges while that possibility remained open.

There may have been an additional reason for Riel's cool reception of the American envoy. A few days before Stutsman's arrival, Begg had noted a growing suspicion in the settlement that mail passing through Pembina was being interfered with:

A great many complaints... from every quarter... that letters coming in have been tampered with – and suspicion is aroused that letters going out are stopped somewhere. The locality of this grievance is not known but it is suspected to be Pembina. Some say McDougall bribed the mailman when he was at Pembina and that through this means he got access to the letters. Others strongly suspect Stutsman and Cavalier the latter the postmaster at Pembina. It will yet come out where this great wrong has been done to a people and who by.[130]

He made another entry to the same effect the day Stutsman returned to Pembina.[131] Shortly after his return, Stutsman wrote a rather plaintive letter to Riel containing what may have been a reference to the postal problems:

I have but a moment in which to write you and beg you to believe that my heart is with your people. If it shall appear that one of our citizens has been playing traitor, it will be made rather warm for him here – rest assured of that.[132]

In a book written years later, Alexander Begg claimed that the mail tamperer was subsequently discovered to be W.B. O'Donoghue.[133] It was certainly an act of which O'Donoghue was capable. It would also have been quite in character for Enos Stutsman. If he escaped ultimate blame for interfering with Riel's communications, he seems never to have recovered the trust which the Métis leaders placed in him during the early stages of the uprising.

Indeed, Stutsman had by now become a target of derision in some parts of the settlement. When the desirability of a rail line to Pembina was being discussed at a public meeting at the end of January, one of the speakers commented sardonically that "the only use would be to bring Stutsman to Fort Garry... "[134] Shortly before that, Stutsman had been threatened with tar and feathering the next time he visited the settlement. He mentioned this in a letter to Begg, enquiring cockily about the price of tar and feathers, and adding that if he were so treated, "there may be a few thousand of his countrymen wanting the same." Begg's comment was, "It is a pity if there are a few thousand like him in the U.S."[135] On another occasion Begg described "some of the measures proposed" by Stutsman as "diabolical in the extreme, and unmentionable here."[136] Deputy Collector Nelson reported to Washington in February that he had evidence that Stutsman and Cavalier had been pointed out to Sioux Indians by Canadians as the first Americans to attack if hostilities arose.[137]

Stutsman's journalistic partner, Henry Robinson, was also encountering increasing opposition to his pro-American editorials in the *New Nation*. Riel's disapproval finally forced a change of tune, and, in mid-March, Robinson's resignation.[138] Presumably Stutsman's investment in the paper, if any, was withdrawn at the same time.

The pressure was not entirely one-sided; Joseph Lemay was threatened with lynching at one point in his anti-annexation campaign.[139] Lemay and his allies were ultimately successful, however, in bringing about negotiations with Canada. Less than a week after Stutsman returned to Pembina, Donald Smith debated the future of the settlement with Riel and other community leaders at a marathon two-day open air meeting. Although suspicion crackled like frost when the speeches began, and tension remained high throughout, the meeting resulted in agreement to elect another all-settlement convention which, in turn, successfully formulated a common list of demands. A three-man delegation was chosen to negotiate the demands with Canada, and a slightly altered version of Riel's provisional government was authorized to administer the settlement in the interim. These developments quickly replaced the prospect of American annexation as a major topic of discussion.

Other exciting events were occurring as well. Several of Riel's prisoners had escaped from their cells in Fort Garry. Some of them joined other Canadian sympathizers in an abortive coup, and were recaptured shortly after the convention completed its deliberations. One of the prisoners, Thomas Scott, so provoked the wrath of his captors by insulting and obstructive behavior, that he was "tried" for "insubordination" by a rebel tribunal, and stupidly put to death. The escaped Canadian leader John Schultz was on his way to Ontario, where he would exploit Scott's killing to stoke fires of racial and religious hatred that would blaze for years to come.

Annexation sentiment south of the international border had not died down. American newspapers continued to print articles and letters about the threat of Indian warfare breaking out and spreading southward (although a letter from Winnipeg, published in the St. Paul *Pioneer* in Feburary pointed out that "there has not been a winter since I have been here that the Indians have been more quiet and peaceable"[140]). Continued support for annexation in Rupert's Land was assumed.[141] The St. Paul *Daily Press* predicted that within ten years, "Gen. Riel or our friend Enos Stutzman (sic), or perhaps both, will be Senators or members of Congress from the State of Winnipeg."[142] While Stutsman seems to have understood the realities of the situation by this point, many of his compatriots did not. United States Consul Oscar Malmros had been sending intensely pro-annexation reports to Washington, and anonymous annexationist articles to Amercian newspapers.[143] The very day Stutsman left Winnipeg in disappointment, Malmros wrote to Senator Ramsey stressing the strength of annexation feelings within the settlement, and urging the senator to obtain financial assistance from the United States ($25,000 at once, and another $75,000 by May 1) for Riel.[144] The next day, Ramsey had a meeting about the insurrection with President Grant and the secretary of state.[145] Two weeks later he successfully introduced a resolution in the Senate calling upon its Committee on Foreign Relations to consider the expediency of American "mediation" in the dispute.[146] Although the resolution spoke only of mediation, Ramsey's lengthy speech in support of the measure called for an election at which the residents of Rupert's Land (and British Columbia) could decide whether to join Canada or the United States. It also urged an exchange with Canada of this "barren and burdensome possession... separated... by an impassable wilderness of seven hundred miles" for a new reciprocal trade agreement between Canada and the United States.[147]

It was very difficult at the time – and it still is – to judge the extent to which the Grant administration shared the views or encouraged the activities of people like Ramsey, Malmros and Stutsman. There can be little doubt that Washington maintained an avid interest in Rupert's Land events, and would have welcomed the territory if it could have been obtained without undue effort or risk. The attention paid to J.W. Taylor's exhaustive intelligence reports bears witness to that. However, the adventurous William Seward was no longer in charge of American foreign policy, and the "manifest destiny" ideal was not being advanced quite as vigorously as before. The State Department remained, to the annoyance of Consul Oscar Malmros, completely unresponsive to the political content of his reports.[148] There is no record, either, of any official sanction for the initiatives of Senator Ramsey or of Enos Stutsman. While it is true that Ramsey discussed the matter with the secretary of state and the president from time to time, it is likely that he was seeking their support, rather than *vice versa*. When Taylor wrote to the secretary of state about Stutsman's January visit to Winnipeg, he found it necessary to explain to the secretary who Stutsman was.[149] It seems probable, therefore, that Stutsman and the others who publicly supported annexation were acting without official sanction, although the United States Government would undoubtedly have been quick to acknowledge their efforts had they been successful.

If the Grant administration was seriously interested in annexation, it blundered badly in the manner in which it responded to the

22. Oscar Malmros,
first U.S. Consul at Winnipeg

Senate's request to provide it with information about the insurrection. Included among the documents published in compliance with the request was a report by Oscar Malmros, dated September 11, in which he had not only lobbied for annexation, but had confided that the Catholic clergy and officials of the Hudson's Bay Company were opposed to Canadian rule.[150] When a copy of the published report reached Winnipeg on March 14, Malmros concluded that it would be "entirely untenable, impracticable and in fact intolerable" for him to remain in the settlement.[151] He fled the next day, without even taking the time to write a letter of resignation. In a hurried note to Ramsey he commented, "I am astonished that the Department didn't see the impropriety of publishing the letter."[152] The incident contributed materially to a hardening of anti-Americanism among the residents of Rupert's Land. This attitude was expressed, for example, in Riel's "Proclamation to the People of the North West" in May: "If ever the time should unhappily come when another division should take place amongst us, *such as foreigners heretofore sought to create,* that will be the signal for all the disasters which we have had the happiness to avoid."[153]

It was, perhaps, to atone for this blunder, and to keep the door to annexation slightly ajar, that the United States Government then committed an act of overt interference in the rebellion. McDougall had left a shipment of arms and ammunition at Fort Abercrombie for safekeeping. They were intended for government use at Fort Garry, and he had feared that they might be seized by Riel if not protected. Now, on May 25, the secretary of the Treasury Department wrote to the secretary of state as follows:

Arms and ammunition detained at Fort Abercrombie by the Collector of Customs at Pembina on their way to the Selkirk settlement.

The collector at Pembina has been instructed to permit the articles referred to to go forward to their destination without further delay.[154]

Neither the sender nor the recipient of this communication would have been unaware that a rebel regime awaited at the "destination." Nor could they have overlooked the fact that a Canadian military force was preparing to march to the settlement across the wild precambrian shield, ostensibly to ensure an orderly transition to constitutional government,[155] but in reality to avenge the death of Thomas Scott. If the rebels chose to resist the Canadian troops, McDougall's arms would be very useful. At about the same time, the American Government finally acted upon the long-standing requests of Enos Stutsman and others for the establishment of a military outpost near Pembina.[156]

It was now really too late to consider annexation seriously, however. Negotiations between the Government of Canada and the Rupert's Land delegates had, after a shaky beginning, succeeded. The Parliament of Canada enacted legislation granting provincial status, together with most of the other rights demanded, to the new Province of Manitoba. Although American visitors to Winnipeg (influenced, no doubt by the Emmerling Hotel set) continued to report that Riel secretly favored annexation, and would eventually lead the territory into the United States union,[157] the opinion at Pembina was unanimously to the contrary.[158] Enos Stutsman knew that the annexation adventure was over.

Had the adventure succeeded, Enos Stutsman would be regarded as a major figure of American history today. One historian has commented: "He could have become an American hero if Washington had been less timid. If the United States had acquired the British Northwest, an area larger than that of the Louisiana Purchase, he would have done as much as anyone to bring it about...."[159]

What had Stutsman really hoped to accomplish by his frenetic attempts at international intrigue? If all he sought was, as some have suggested, American military protection for Pembina, he was completely successful. J.W. Taylor reported in November, after arriving in Winnipeg via Pembina to take up the consular position Malmros had abandoned: "Pembina is all action with the construction of the post, and railroad prospects... The uncertainty at Red River is sending many to the valley of the Pembina, and a great many settlements between Pembina and St. Joseph may be expected next summer."[160] If he genuinely sought personal fame and fortune through annexation, as he probably did at one level of his complex mentality, he must have been disappointed. There is evidence, however, that at least some of his motivation was idealistic. In a private letter written in June to former Governor Faulk, Stutsman attempted to assess the success of the insurrection:

With reference to the frequent mention of my name in connection with Winnipeg affairs, I will simply say that while I endorse the movement, and from the first have enjoyed a liberal share of the confidence of the Red River people and Government, I have studiously endeavored to keep myself in the background in order to avoid notoriety. That the cause should command respect abroad, it was necessary to have it publicly understood that it was sustained any directed by *native* brain – hence for the sake of the cause – I have been sorry to see my name connected therewith.

Of late I receive many letters enquiring – "What is the situation?" "Is the Winnipeg rising a fizzle?" And as some such questions may enter your mind, I will answer – that thus far the movement has been a success. Never before have a handful of people gained so glorious a victory at so small a cost of blood and treasure.

Had no uprising taken place, McDougall and his staff of hungry officials would have assumed possession. And not a solitary right of the people would have been respected. But – 15,000 people rose and expelled the Canadian hirelings, assumed the right of temporary self-government, and what have they accomplished? The Dominion, with a population of seven millions, has passed an Act granting their demands, and if matters are thus adjusted, the Red River people will have received the right of self-government, and *far* more money than the United States or any other government, *save* Canada, *would* have given. These terms, if unaccompanied by an armed force, will of course be accepted. But as Canada still seems to be advancing her troops as an army of invasion, the people are induced to doubt the good faith of that government, surmising that said act of parliament was a mere sham to lull the Winnipeggers... If these troops continue to advance, and if the very best guarantees of their good intentions be not given, they will be met in the swamps and lagoons, in which case a collision will be inevitable.

But I cannot believe that the Canadian Government is so mad as to drive a brave people to desperation. I therefore regard the question the same as settled. You will therefore perceive that *Riel* has not backed down in the least. And that by a *bold* stroke 15,000 people have secured self-government, and millions of money and land.[161]

Even when it is acknowledged that at this point Stutsman probably still had his eye on some of the money and land referred to, this is not the letter of a man who was wholly motivated by personal gain.

The Red River insurrection was not yet over. Stutsman would have further occasion to play minor roles in it and in its aftermath, but his attention had by this time reverted to matters south of the international boundary.

CHAPTER SIX

THE FINAL CHAPTER
1870-1874

STUTSMAN TOOK A VACATION IN THE SUM-
mer of 1870. The *Sioux City Times* recorded in July that "Col. E.
Stutsman, the hero of numerous Red River exploits, is stopping
at the Northwestern."[1] The *Yankton Press* noted, a couple of weeks
later, that he was "revisiting the scenes of days long since departed,"
and went on to remark that "he still retains his bouyancy of spirits,
robust health and intellectual vigor, notwithstanding the exciting
events with which he has been connected... in what is known as the
Red River Rebellion, which is now happily closed in the interests of
freedom and humanity."[2]

When he returned to Pembina in early September he learned that
the troubles in Manitoba were in fact far from "happily closed." During his absence the Canadian troops had arrived in Winnipeg after a
summer-long wilderness trek. Riel and his followers had offered no
resistance; they had in fact planned a welcoming ceremony. However,
as the troops approached Winnipeg it was learned that they were in a
belligerent mood, and the rebel leaders were accordingly forced to flee

23. Enos Stutsman

at the last minute to the sanctuary of the United States. Louis Riel and Ambroise Lépine were now at St. Joseph's, west of Pembina, and O'Donoghue, the Fenian enthusiast, was staying in Pembina. In Winnipeg the troops has released the pent-up frustrations of their arduous journey, as well as their festering desire to avenge the death of Thomas Scott, with an orgy of dissipation and persecution of suspected rebel sympathizers.[3] A member of the Métis tribunal that condemned Scott had been stoned and drowned,[4] and a number of prominent Winnipeg Americans had fled.[5]

The exiled Métis leaders were so distressed about these developments that they slipped back across the boundary on September 17, and held a meeting at St. Norbert with some of their confreres who had remained in Manitoba. They agreed on a "memorial and petition" addressed to the president of the United States, asking him to use his good offices to ensure that the Métis grievances would be remedied. Riel and O'Donoghue differed sharply and angrily over the contents of the document. O'Donoghue insisted that it include a request for American annexation of the territory, but Riel was able, after intense debate, to convince a majority of those present at the meeting that no reference should be made to annexation.

Despite his opposition to the form of the memorial, O'Donoghue was commissioned to present it to President Grant. When he arrived back at Pembina after the meeting (Riel and Lépine having returned to St. Joseph's), he took the document to Enos Stutsman, who concurred in his objections to its form. Without consulting any of the Métis leaders, the two men revised the memorial to include references to the possibility of annexation. The major alteration was a new paragraph calling for steps that would enable the population of the area to "enjoy the blessings of life, liberty, property, and the pursuit of happiness, under a Government of our own choice, or in union with a people with whom we think we can enjoy these blessings."[6] Some of the language of the paragraph was taken directly from Senator Ramsey's "mediation" speech in February, a move no doubt intended to flatter Ramsey and to secure his assistance in approaching the president. In this they were successful, but, despite Ramsey's support, O'Donoghue was unable when he arrived in Washington to induce President Grant to become embroiled in the affair. The United States Government seems by that time to have abandoned the possibility of annexation. The northern plains would remain Canadian.

Stutsman remained interested in developments in the new Canadian province of Manitoba, but his attitude became more detached than previously. In December, when elections were in the offing in Manitoba, he wrote to J.W. Taylor in Winnipeg, offering some quite perceptive observations about the state of political affairs in the northern settlement. He predicted election violence (an accurate prophesy), and suggested that "should Canuck, English and Half-Breed blood flow to the saddle-skirt, I trust you will have the prudence to seek protection beneath the ample folds of the American flag."[7] With one minor exception, Stutsman was himself to remain in the shelter of the American flag for the rest of his life.

Although these events momentarily redirected Stutsman's attention to affairs north of the border, his chief interest after returning from vacation was a new position to which he had just been appointed by the United States Government: register of the newly created United States Land Office at Pembina. After numerous requests by Stutsman and others, the government had finally authorized the establishment of a registry for the orderly distribution of public land, by sale as well as by pre-emption and homestead claims. Stutsman's appointment as the first register at an annual salary of $500,[8] seems to have been a reward for his efforts during the Riel Rebellion. Writing to a friend in June, before the Senate had approved the appointment, he commented:

Thanks for your congratulations – but as I have not been yet advised of my confirmation, I shall not be at all surprised if the Senate would deem such confirmation an official endorsement of my Winnipeg record, affording Canada ground upon which to base a Declaration of War!![9]

He went on to say, "As I did not *ask* for the office, do not *need* it and am fast growing old and lazy, I do not trouble my brain about what the Senate may or may not do." Such disclaimers of personal interest were typical of Stutsman, and it is difficult to believe that someone as keenly interested in real estate speculation as Stutsman was would not have

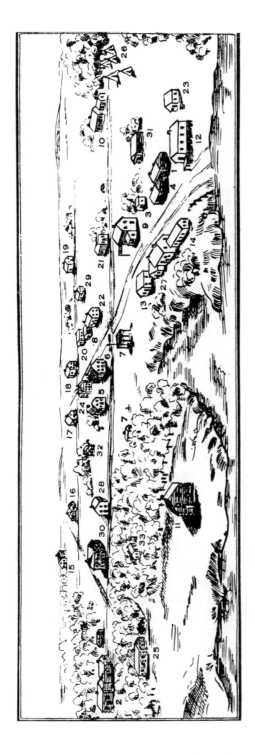

24. Pembina, D.T., in the early 1870s. Cavalier residence and post office, 2. Joseph Rolette residence, 24. Stutsman Building, 3o. Saloons, 4, 5, 8, 12, 13, and 22. The sketch is credited to Frank A. Wardwell, the first school teacher in the area, and is thought to have been made at the time. One source dates it in the 1860s, but Stutsman's building was not constructed until 1871.

regarded the appointment as a valuable plum. It offered information and influence that could be turned to personal profit. There is no evidence, however, that Stutsman ever took improper advantage of his position as register. He never obtained personal pre-emption or homestead grants at Pembina (he would have been legally precluded from doing so by his continued ownership of land in Yankton), and he never purchased any public land in the area. It is true that the first pre-emption grants were made to his cronies Joe Rolette Sr. and Charles Cavalier, and that Stutsman bought half interests in both grants shortly after they were made;[10] but since Rolette and Cavalier were among the earliest residents of Pembina it is not surprising that they made the first claims. Stutsman would probably have collaborated with them regardless of who had been in charge of the land office.

There were some who suspected Stutsman of attempting to use his position as land register for personal gain in connection with Métis land claims. A Washington judge, R.F. Crowell, was sent to the area in the fall of 1870, apparently at the urging of Senator Ramsey, to enumerate such claims. These were assertions of aboriginal land rights by persons of Indian ancestry who, by reason of mixed blood, were not entitled to live on Indian reserve lands. The government was considering the distribution of land or land vouchers (scrip) to Métis residents in settlement of these claims. In a letter to Ramsey in October, Crowell complained that the new land register was being obstructive. Stutsman had objected to an enumeration being made, and had contended that these claims should be handled, like all other claims to public land, through his office. This was a justifiable position. The Métis were mobile people, and a once-for-always enumeration by a visiting official would inevitably exclude many valid claims by persons not in the district at the time. Crowell's visit occurred during hunting season. Moreover, the resident land register would be a better qualified judge of the validity of claims than any itinerant enumerator. In resisting Crowell's efforts, Stutsman was simply following instructions that had been issued by his department to administer Métis claims in the same manner as all others.

Crowell suspected, however, that Stutsman had ulterior motives:

Now you can readily perceive what a chance there is for a speculation if a man is disposed to make one, and it is said that Stutsman has ready money and is worth... $150,000. There are many half-breeds in this region, and many more come roaming through here... (I)t is an easy matter for interested parties to fix up these half-breeds to come into a land office and make application whether they are entitled or not and then at the same time... they will sell it, to these same parties, for a small sum. With an open field as to number and an indefinite time... many hundred could be manipulated.[11]

The report that Enos Stutsman was worth $150,000 was absurd – at least in terms of "ready money." His own estimate of his worth that fall for the United States decennial census was $30,000 in realty and $500 in personalty.[12] The fear that he would use his position to profit from Métis land rights, though more plausible, turned out to be equally false. Crowell did not succeed in having a special procedure established for the Métis claims; they continued to be handled like all other claims, as Stutsman had insisted. Yet Stutsman did not purchase any land from roving Métis; all the property he ever owned in the Pembina area was purchased from Rolette, Cavalier, and another prominent Pembina resident, William Moorhead.[13]

That winter was relatively quiet – devoted primarily to completing the organization of the land office and recording the flurry of pre-emption and homestead applications that its establishment prompted. Stutsman chose not to run in the first biennial election for the Territorial Legislature, probably because his duties as land register would not permit it. In the campaign for territorial delegate to Congress he switched allegiance from Spink back to his old colleague Walter Burleigh, but both men were defeated by Democrat M.K. Armstrong.[14] The Armstrong victory would not have troubled Stutsman much, however; he and Armstrong had been warm friends since the early days of Yankton.

The 1870-71 session of the Territorial Legislature had designated Pembina as a judicial center, and in June 1871, the first court sitting was held.[15] Enos Stutsman did not appear as counsel at that session, probably because of the paucity of cases (one report said that only one case was tried). He was present for the occasion, however – as foreman of the grand jury. A Yankton newspaper later claimed that the sole case on the docket was a charge of timber theft against the jury foreman, but this was indignantly denied by the clerk of the court.[16]

The rumored timber theft may have been linked in some way with a construction project Stutsman had under way. Now that the district was showing signs of a coming boom, he was anxious to get back into the real estate business on as large a scale as possible, and he would need proper business premises. The coming of the court to Pembina had also created a need for courtroom facilities. Stutsman decided, therefore, to construct a two-storey building that could serve both purposes: real estate office on the main floor, courtrooms above. When the court authorities agreed to rent the space from him, he made arrangements for the construction of what would be Pembina's most substantial building up to that time.[17]

Since the operation of a real estate business would not be compatible with holding the position of United States land register, Stutsman resigned the position in the summer of 1871. Then, having nothing much to do while his building was under construction, he decided to take another vacation trip to Yankton.

It seems to have been a very pleasant journey. Upon his return to Pembina in September he wrote to a friend in Yankton reporting his safe arrival and commenting that the growth of railway lines had now reduced the travelling distance between the two places to only 1,163 miles each way. It was an odd letter, written in a less legible hand than normal, and considerably more personal in content than usual. It may have been written under the mellowing influence of alcohol. It expressed considerable optimism: Fort Pembina would be finished by winter, his real estate office would open in October, and "the future looks bright, our people love God, fear the Devil, and keep themselves unspotted from the world." But the tone was melancholy. The reason appeared toward the end of the letter:

O how fondly my heart turns to the loved ones of the St. Charles – and I daresay if the bright smiles of the beautiful Annie had dawned upon me my said heart would at this time be a fixture in and about that hotel. But so hath it been decreed that said smiles are to be lavished upon a "Hans." Hans – thou vainglorious, blind old fool – the "Little God" showers his favors upon thee and thou knoweth it not. Awake, arise, awake. And make hay while the sun shineth![18]

Enos was forty-five years old (though he had admitted to being only forty in the previous year's census), and still a bachelor. It is unlikely, in spite of his disability, that he lived a wholly celibate life. Joseph Lemay had claimed in a letter to Bishop Taché during the Riel Rebellion that Stutsman and Rolette had three gods: "money, women and public schools,"[19] Nevertheless, he must have felt keenly the absence of a permanent female partner. His whimsical manner in the letter fails to conceal a note of desperation.

He was in the process of moving into his new office building and getting business under way when an event occurred which again focussed his attention on Manitoba. W.B. O'Donoghue, having failed to convince President Grant to undertake annexation, had turned his efforts to the Fenian Brotherhood, headquartered in New York. When that organization withheld support, O'Donoghue privately raised a tiny ragtag force and, on October 5, launched an "invasion" of Manitoba from Pembina. The invading "army" consisted of about thirty-five men, a few of whom were Fenians. They acted without official Fenian approval, however. The raiders got no further than the Hudson's Bay Company post at North Pembina, where they were dispersed, and their leaders arrested, by a force of United States soldiers from the newly-established Fort Pembina.[20]

Before he realized how laughable the "invasion" threat really was, the new lieutenant governor of Manitoba, Adams Archibald, issued a call to arms, ordering an enumeration of all able-bodied men in the settlement. On the day after the O'Donoghue foray, the deputy collector of Canadian customs at North Pembina complied with the lieutenant governor's order by enlisting every man in the vicinity, including some Indians who worked at the Hudson's Bay Company post. And who should be watching as he did so but Enos Stutsman? What Stutsman was doing there is anybody's guess. He had been retained as defence counsel for some of the arrested "invaders," so he may have come to North Pembina to gather evidence about the previous day's events. In any case, Stutsman immediately protested the enlistment of Indians. Receiving no satisfaction from Canadian officials on the scene, he swore a deposition as to what he had observed, and caused it to be forwarded to Lieutenant Governor Archibald, along with an indignant protest.[21] As it happened, the lieutenant governor had learned independently of the recruitment of Indians, and, being a much wiser man than governor-designate McDougall, had already ordered that they be excluded.[22]

At the initial hearing of the arrested invaders, Stutsman had his first opportunity to appear in a professional capacity in the courtroom he owned and rented to the government. It was a successful appearance; he and co-counsel George Potter managed to have all the prisoners released.[23] When Winnipeg lawyer J.F. Bain arrived in Pembina ("that little hell-hole") to attempt the extradition of O'Donoghue, he found the lock-up empty. He did catch a glimpse of his prey on the street ("... a more villainous looking wretch it has never been my misfortune to see. His appearance would hang him in any well-regulated community... "), but the swiftness of Stutsman's legal maneuvers had precluded the possibility of extradition.[24]

Stutsman did not participate in the case when it was retried at higher judicial levels. In fact, his only further involvement with the "Fenian raid," or with Manitoba affairs at all, was to gather and pass on to Taylor certain evidence to the effect that a man arrested and tried by Canadian authorities in connection with the incursion had been taken into custody on United States soil.[25] The case was very controversial, and seemed for a time to endanger American–Canadian relations,[26] but Stutsman's role in it appears to have been minor. With the knowledge that Manitoba was now on the road to effective democratic government, and that Washington no longer had any inclination to a Canadian adventure, his interest in affairs north of the border had evaporated.

Although Pembina was still a long way from being a boom town, the real estate business burgeoned satisfactorily during the winter of 1871–72. In March the property which Stutsman owned in partnership with the Cavaliers and Mrs. Rolette (Joe Sr. having died) was surveyed into town lots, and a subdivision plan was filed with the register of deeds.[27] This was followed by an extremely complex series of conveyances, all filed the same day, which had the effect of distributing individual ownership of the lots among the former partners (as well as William Moorhead, who also had an interest in property covered by the plan.)[28] It must have taken Stutsman weeks to prepare the conveyance documents. There then followed a string of sales by Stutsman and the others to various purchasers. By the end of the year Stutsman had recovered from fifteen sales the full amount of his investment, and still owned many more lots in the townsite than anyone else.

There is a legend that Pembina's original landowners played poker for the ownership of town lots. The story may be rooted in the apparently haphazard blizzard of conveyances filed on March 4, 1872. However, when the entire transaction is analyzed carefully it can be seen to be a rational, if complicated, scheme for converting the common interests of the former partners to individually owned and equitably distributed holdings. It is entirely possible that some of the subsequent transactions were based on the fall of playing cards. In fact, given the nature of the community, the long cold winter evenings, and the abundance of available real property, one is tempted to regard it as probable. There were a few "sales" recorded for unusually low prices.[29] For the most part, however, the land transfers in which Enos Stutsman was involved appear to have been legitimate business transactions.

One of the self-indulgences of the original filers of the town plan was to name the streets of their hoped-for metropolis after themselves. Strollers along Stutsman Street in modern Pembina should not suppose that the name was bestowed by a grateful community in recognition of Enos Stutsman's many accomplishments; he chose it himself. He was careful, also, to include the names of individuals who, like Senator Ramsey of Minnesota, might be useful to him in the future. Not long after, Stutsman and another early Dakota resident were chiefly responsible for the selection of the names for several new Dakota counties. Stutsman County was among them.[30]

When the biennial election for the Territorial Legislature was held in late 1871, Enos Stutsman decided that it was time to enter the political arena once more. He had time on his hands again, and perhaps he was yearning for the comparatively bright lights of Yankton. He won election to the Territorial Council handily, and when he entered the council chamber in late December, after an almost four-year absence, he was immediately chosen president.[31]

One of Stutsman's first legislative acts was to move the adoption of a memorial to Congress calling for the division of Dakota into two separate territories. No one knew better than he did the enormous obstacles to transportation and communication between the northern and southern sections of the Territory, and the gulf in understanding that resulted from them. Now that the northern areas were becoming more populous, it was time, he thought, that the north had an indigenous government. Absentee government was, after all, one of the causes of the rebellion that had recently flared in neighboring Manitoba. Stutsman's memorial, which was quickly passed, was not the first to be adopted by the Territorial Legislature. A similar request had been made to Congress by the previous legislature, but had been turned down. This memorial met with a similar fate in Washington, as, indeed, did several later attempts. The division of Dakota was not achieved until many years after Stutsman's death. He is, nevertheless, regarded as the father of the idea. In a lengthy newspaper account of the division movement, two of the Territory's earliest politicians, both of whom had become respected historians, credited Stutsman with originating the scheme – long before he introduced the 1872 memorial. M.K. Armstrong, who had the responsibility, as territorial delegate to Congress, of trying to sell the idea in Washington, recalled that Stutsman had convinced him as early as 1867, when the two men rode southward across the prairie after Stutsman's first election as a representative from Pembina:

... all through those... long days and nights of riding and camping, Stutsman's ever-recurring conversation was upon the pressing need for a separate territorial organization for the "new empire" up in northern Dakota. He would then nudge me in the ribs, pull out his historic flask, and suggest that the day would come when he and I would go to Congress as the Delegates from North and South Dakota.[32]

It was, as it turned out, Stutsman's last crusade. Near the end of the session, in January 1873, he was taken ill with a bronchial infection. For some reason his normally robust constitution was unable to throw off the infection, and he remained in bed in Yankton, unimproved, throughout the spring and summer. In September he decided

66

The will mentioned of Enos Stutsman
deceased in the foregoing is in words
and figures as follows, to wit:

I, Enos Stutsman, of the County of Pembina
and Territory of Dakota being of sound
mind and memory do make publish and
declare this my last will and testament
in manner following:

<u>First</u> I give devise and bequeath to
Charles Cavalier and Isabella
Cavalier his wife of the County of
Pembina and Territory of Dakota
all and singular my personal
property baggage and effects
of every nature and kind whatsoever

<u>Second</u> I give devise and bequeath unto
John B. Charles, of Sioux City Iowa
and to his heirs and assigns forever
all that tract or parcel of land
lying and being in the County of
Pembina and Territory of Dakota
described as follows, to wit: The West
half of the South East quarter
of Section number five (5) in
Township number one hundred
and sixty three (163) North of
Range number fifty one (51)
West of the fifth principal meridian
containing eighty acres of land
according to the Government
survey thereof

<u>Third</u> I give devise and bequeath unto
my niece Mary Stutsman of
Princeton in the State of Arkansas
and unto John B. Charles of
Sioux City of the State of Iowa
and to their heirs and assigns

testament.
In witness whereof I have

25. Official copy of the will of Enos Stutsman, January 22, 1874

to risk the journey home, and made the long painful trip accompanied by a friend. It was an unwise move; by the time he reached Pembina his condition was much worse.[33] He had been appointed register of deeds for Pembina County[34] (a different position from his previous one as register of land), but his health would not permit him to carry out the duties of the office.

As winter descended on Pembina he continued to deteriorate, and by mid-January he knew that it was time to put his affairs in order. This he did, despite his weakened condition, with characteristic thoroughness and thoughtfulness. In a carefully drafted will, he left certain real property to a niece in Arkansas and to an old friend, John Charles, in Sioux City, a monetary bequest to the daughter of another old friend in Yankton, and his cash and personal property to the Cavaliers.[35] All of his remaining real property in Pembina he "sold" to the Cavaliers for a probably fictitious sum, rather than devise it to them. This may have been done to save them the complication and delay of having to wait for the probate of his will before dealing with the land.[36]

Two days after these arrangements were completed, on January 24, 1874, Enos Stutsman died.

A man who had known him well, often as a political opponent, wrote the following at the time of Stutsman's death:

It is claimed that nature is fond of compensations, and what the good dame had denied to Mr. Stutsman physically she had made up in other favors. No doubt his physical inability to pursue the great majority of avocations, taken in connection with his genial and obliging disposition, won him the good will of the people; but had be been less competent, less a leader, less able, he could not have attained the position among his fellows which he occupied and maintained.

Mr. Stutsman was fond of the sunshine, and his disposition and temperament were in fellowship with this fondness. He was a most companionable gentleman, genial, generous, never giving offense, and the life of the social circle. Among the pioneers of the Missouri slope, it was said that Stutsman could, in cases of political emergency, muster the most numerous personal clan of any leader in the territory.[37]

NOTES

PROLOGUE

1. W.L. Morton (ed.), *The Red River Journal of Alexander Begg* (1956), p. 259. This entry was dated January 12, 1870, but the same journal also recorded Stutsman's and Lemay's arrivals on January 9, which would seem from other evidence to have been the correct date.

2. The fullest previous account was an unpublished Master's thesis: Marjorie A. Stoa, *Enos Stutsman: Influential Pioneer, Dakota Territory, 1858–1874*, North Dakota State University, 1962. Briefer descriptions of or references to Stutsman can be found in a variety of published sources, some of which are much more reliable than others. Among the more dependable are: H. Bowsfield, "Enos Stutsman," *Dictionary of Canadian Biography*, vol. X, 1972; John K. Howard, *The Strange Empire of Louis Riel* (1952), pp. 76ff (a brief and undocumented, but accurate and well-written description); and G.W. Kingsbury, *History of Dakota Territory* (1915). Although Stutsman's real nature and accomplishments are obscured by legend and hearsay in some accounts (e.g.: "A Gaety of History," *Monthly South Dakotan*, August 1901, p.111; A.C. Gluek, *Minnesota and the Manifest Destiny of the Canadian Northwest* [1965], p. 265; B. Willson, *The Life of Lord Strathcona and Mount Royal* [1915], p. 291), his one appearance in outright fiction – as "Mr. Shorthorn" in Alexander Begg's long-forgotten novel of the Canadian northwest, *Dot It Down* (1871) – is a quite accurate, if unflattering, word sketch by one who knew him.

CHAPTER ONE

1. *Dakotian*, Yankton, D.T., Dec. 23, 1862. This sketch, presumably based on an interview with Stutsman, is the most reliable source of information available on the man, though

it provides only rudimentary information; John Hale Stutsman Jr., *Jacob Stützman (? -1773): His Children and Grandchildren* (1982). The latter source indicates that the year the family was established in America may have been 1726.

2. G.W. Kingsbury, "Enos Stutsman," *Collections of the State Historical Society of North Dakota,* I(1906), p.350. An obituary in the *Sioux City Journal,* Feb. 10, 1874, stated that Stutsman was born January 29, 1826.
3. *Dakotian,* Dec. 23, 1862. The Polk County (Des Moines) Recorder's Office *Land Records,* Book H. 101, indicate a land transaction involving Stutsman dated July 13, 1855.
4. The *Sioux City Journal,* Feb. 10, 1874, comments in Stutsman's obituary notice on the wealth he accumulated during his short time in Des Moines.
5. *Dakotian,* Dec. 23, 1862; Kingsbury, "Enos Stutsman," p.350.
6. *Sioux City Iowa Eagle,* Oct. 31, 1857.
7. *Sioux City Register,* May 5 and 12, 1859.
8. *Sioux City Eagle,* July 4, 1857.
9. Ibid., Aug. 8, 1857. A story about the building in the *Sioux City Daily Times,* Dec. 15, 1869, refers to "the framework of the building being made in St. Louis," and to its erection at the time being "looked upon as a credit to the city."
10. *Sioux City Journal,* June 5, 1924, p.34.
11. *Record Book A,* Iowa 7th District Court, Woodbury County, Dec. 10, 1857, p.37.
12. *Sioux City Journal,* June 5, 1924, p.34.
13. *State of Iowa* v. *Robert Moffatt, Angus McLellan & Elizabeth Smith, Record Book A,* Dec. 10, 1857, p.63.
14. Stutsman sponsored Charles upon his call to the Iowa bar: *Record Book A,* Feb. 20, 1858.
15. The term *Métis* is used throughout the text to describe all people of mixed Indian and white ancestry. The term has evolved over the last hundred years. The English language originally described a person of mixed British and Indian ancestry as *half-breed. Métis* was the term originally used by the French-speaking population in the northwest of North America to describe people of white and Indian ancestry. Gradually the term *Métis* has been used to describe all people in Canada who are of mixed Indian and white ancestry, and it is now considered synonymous with *half-breed.* (D.B. Sealey and A.S. Lussier, *The Metis: Canada's Forgotten People* [1975], pp.1 and 2.)
16. *Annals of Iowa,* vol. 8, p.401ff.
17. F.M. Ziebach, "The First Marriage in Dakota Territory," *South Dakota Historical Collections* (1920), pp. 548-51.
18. John F. Schmidt, *A Historical Profile of Sioux City* (1969), p.185.
19. *Annals of Iowa,* vol. 8, p.401ff.
20. *Sioux City Eagle,* Apr. 3, 1858.
21. Schmidt, *Historical Profile,* p.185.
22. The purchaser was his crony John H. Charles. (*Sioux City Eagle,* Jan. 16, 1858.)
23. The City Council building was advertised for sale in the *Sioux City Register* May 5 and 12, 1859.
24. The final advertisement for the law partnership appeared in the June 11, 1859 issue of the *Sioux City Eagle.*

CHAPTER TWO

1. Herbert S. Schell, *Dakota Territory During the 1860's,* Governmental Research Bureau, University of South Dakota (1954), pp.2-4.

Notes

2. Schmidt, *Historial Profile* p.165.
3. R.F. Karolevitz, *Yankton: A Pioneer Past* (1972), p.8.
4. Schell, *Dakota Territory*, p.6.
5. Kingsbury, *History of Dakota Territory* vol. I, p.117.
6. *Dakotian*, Dec. 23, 1862.
7. Kingsbury, "Enos Stutsman," pp.350-54.
8. *Sioux City Journal*, Feb. 10, 1874; *Dakota Herald*, Yankton, D.T., Feb. 3, 1874.
9. Schell, *Dakota Territory*, pp.6-8.
10. Moses Armstrong in the *Dakota Union*, July 5, 1864.
11. Schell, *Dakota Territory*, pp.8-9.
12. Karolevitz, *Pioneer Past*, p.4.
13. Ibid.
14. Schell, *Dakota Territory*, p.17ff.
15. Karolevitz, *Pioneer Past*, p.16.
16. Ibid., p.15.
17. *Weekly Dakotian*, Aug. 5, 1862.
18. *Sioux City Register*, Jan. 21, 1860.
19. Schell, *Dakota Territory*, p.17. A petition purporting to be signed by all settlers about the same time bore 428 signatures, p.16.
20. G.W. Kingsbury, *South Dakota Historical Collections* (1920), vol. 10.
21. Schell, *Dakota Territory*, p.29.
22. Karolevitz, *Pioneer Past*, p.7.
23. Moses K. Armstrong, quoted in Schell, *Dakota Territory*, p.16.
24. Karolevitz, *Pioneer Past*, p.20.
25. Kingsbury, "Enos Stutsman"; H.R. Lamar, *Dakota Territory 1861–1889* (1956), p.82.
26. *Weekly Dakotian*, June 6, 1861.
27. Although land records for the earliest years do not appear to exist, some indication of the extent of Stutsman's Yankton holdings can be derived from a list of unpaid land taxes in 1874. (*Dakota Herald*, Jan. 27, 1874.) Even then, after much of his choice property would have been sold, 85 lots and five entire blocks remained in his name.
28. *Record Book A*, Dec. 13, 1858.
29. *Weekly Dakotian*, July 27, 1861.
30. Moses K. Armstrong, *The Early Empire Builders of the West* (1901), p.32.
31. Karolevitz, *Pioneer Past*, p.27.
32. "Log Roller" (later identified as Moses K. Armstrong), *Sioux City Register* Apr. 22, 1862.
33. Ibid., May 8, 1862.
34. Karolevitz, *Pioneer Past*, p.29, quoting an eye-witness, F.M. Ziebach: *South Dakota Historical Collections* (1920), vol. 10.
35. Lamar, *Dakota Territory 1861–1889*, p.82.
36. Karolevitz, *Pioneer Past*, p.29.
37. Armstrong, *Early Empire Builders*, p.67.
38. Schell, *Dakota Territory*, p.63.
39. *Dakotian*, Dec. 23, 1862.
40. Kingsbury, *History of Dakota Territory*, p.463.
41. Armstrong, *Sioux City Register*, Apr. 20, 1862.
42. Karolevitz, *Pioneer Past*, pp.31-32.
43. Armstrong, *Sioux City Register*, Apr. 22, 1862, quoted in Karolevitz, *Pioneer Past*, p.31.

44. Jayne to Stutsman, June 30, 1863, Jayne Papers, *Dakota Territorial Records*, Reel 16.
45. Schell, *Dakota Territory*, p.47.
46. Ibid.
47. Karolevitz, *Pioneer Past*, p.34.
48. Schell, *Dakota Territory*, p.48.
49. Karolevitz, *Pioneer Past*, p.34; Schell, *Dakota Territory*, p.48.
50. Karolevitz, *Pioneer Past*, pp.35–36.
51. Schell, *Dakota Territory*, p.48; Karolevitz *Pioneer Past*, p.36.
52. Schell, *Dakota Territory*, p.48.
53. Karolevitz, *Pioneer Past*, p.37.
54. Armstrong, *Sioux City Register*, Sept. 23, 1862.
55. Karolevitz, *Pioneer Past*, p.32.
56. Ibid, p.38.
57. Stoa, *Enos Stutsman: Influential Pioneer*, p. 10, cites as authority for this version, "Early Guard History," *South Dakota Historical Collections*, vol. VI (1912), p.368.
58. Ibid.
59. A.M. English, *Monthly South Dakotan* (1899–1900), vol. 2, p.199.
60. D. Robinson, *Encyclopaedia of South Dakota* (1925), p.714.
61. Karolevitz, *Pioneer Past*, p.37.
62. Ibid., p.36.
63. Ibid., pp.39–40.
64. *Dakotian*, Dec. 23, 1862.
65. Kingsbury, *History of Dakota Territory*, p.463.
66. Ibid.
67. Jayne to Stutsman, June 30, 1863, Jayne Papers, Reel 16. It is possible that the year was an error in penmanship, and was intended to read "1862."
68. Edmunds to Stutsman, October 7, 1863, Jayne Papers, Reel 16.
69. Stutsman to Edmunds, Oct. 7, 1863, Jayne Papers, Reel 16.
70. Lamar, *Dakota Territory, 1861–1889*, p.97, states that Stutsman was still private secretary to the governor during the 1864–65 legislative session.
71. *Dakotian*, Sept. 15, 1863.
72. Schell, *Dakota Territory*, pp.78–79.
73. Kingsbury, *Pioneer Past*, p.385, states that he was elected to the latter position in October 1864.
74. *Legislative Council Journal*, 4th Session Dakota Territory Legislative Assembly, 1865, pp.172–73.
75. *Dakotian*, May 26, 1863.
76. *Weekly Dakota Union*, Yankton, Aug. 16, 1864.
77. *Union and Dakotian*, Yankton, June 10, 1865.
78. *Dakotian*, Dec. 23, 1862.
79. "A Gaety of History," pp.110–12.
80. *Legislative Council Journal*, pp.6–7.
81. D. Robinson, *History of South Dakota* (1904), vol. I, p.224.
82. Jayne to Lincoln, May 4, 1864, U.S. National Archives, Micro Series M 650, Roll 47, *Letters of Application and Recommendation During Administration of A. Lincoln and A. Johnson, 1861–1869*.
83. Lamar, *Dakota Territory 1861–1889*, p.97.

Notes

84. The governor's Thanksgiving message, Nov., 1865, refers to Spink as the governor's secretary: Jayne Papers, Reel 16.
85. Schell, *Dakota Territory*, p.64.
86. Ibid., p.79.
87. Ibid.
88. Stutsman to Sargent, Feb. 9, 1866, U.S. National Archives, *Bureau of Customs Records*, R.G. 36.
89. Stutsman to Sargent, July 24, 1866 (from Pembina), *Customs Records*, R.G. 36.

CHAPTER THREE

1. The 1850 census indicated more than 1,000: Lamar, *Dakota Territory 1861–1889*, p.51.
2. Ibid., p.53.
3. Ibid., p.52.
4. Ibid., p.86.
5. Ibid., pp.95 and 112.
6. Stutsman to Sargent, Feb. 9, 1866, *Customs Records*, R.G. 36.
7. *Union and Dakotian*, Feb. 17, 1866; Stutsman to Sargent, March 14, 1866, July 31, 1867 and Sept. 26, 1867, *Customs Records* R.G. 36.
8. So described by Joseph Lemay, the customs collector at Pembina. (Lemay to Sargent, Sept. 6, 1866, *Customs Records*, R.G. 36.)
9. Kingsbury, *History of Dakota Territory*, p.95.
10. Stutsman to Sargent, July 24, 1866 and March 18, 1867, *Customs Records*, R.G. 36.
11. James B. Prower, *Collections of the State Historical Society of North Dakota* (1910), vol. III, p.337.
12. G.F.G. Stanley, *Louis Riel* (1972), p.79.
13. G.B. Winship, "Early Politics and Politicians of North Dakota," *U.N.D. Quarterly Journal*, 13(1923), p.260.
14. Lemay to Sargent, Sept. 6, 1866, *Customs Records*, R.G. 36.
15. Stutsman to Sargent, May 15, June 9, Aug. 23, and Dec. 3, 1866, *Customs Records*, R.G. 36.
16. Stutsman to Murray, Mar. 1, 1867, *Customs Records*, R.G. 36.
17. Stutsman to Sargent, Sept. 17, 1866, *Customs Records*, R.G. 36.
18. Stutsman to Secretary of Treasury, Mar. 1, 1867, U.S. National Archives, *Custom House Nominations, Pembina, D.T.*, R.G. 56, Box 379.
19. Stutsman to Murray, Mar. 1, 1867 *Customs Records*, R.G. 36.
20. Ibid., Dec. 10, 1867.
21. Stutsman to Sargent, Dec. 6, 1867, *Customs Records*, R.G. 36.
22. Ibid., Oct. 23, 1868.
23. Stutsman to Secretary of Treasury, Jan. 1, 1867, *Nominations*, R.G. 56, Box 379.
24. Stutsman to Lemay, Oct. 25, 1867, *Nominations*, R.G. 56, Box 379.
25. Lemay to Secretary of Treasury, Nov. 17, 1867, U.S. National Archives, Micro Series 174 (10-51-1), Roll 88, document 139.
26. Stutsman to Sargent, March 13, 1868, *Customs Records*, R.G. 36.
27. Ibid., Oct. 23, 1868.
28. Ibid., Jan. 8, 1868.
29. Ibid., May 20, 1867.
30. Ibid., Dec. 5, 1868.

31. Ibid., Oct. 27, 1868.
32. Armstrong, *Early Empire Builders*, p.53.
33. Stutsman to Sargent, Feb. 22, 1868, *Customs Records*, R.G. 36.
34. Ibid., May 18, 1867.
35. Ibid., Oct. 23, 1868.
36. Ibid.
37. Secretary of Treasury to Lemay, Mar. 29, 1869, and to J.C. Stoever, May 4, 1869, U.S. National Archives, Micro. Series 175 (10-51-5), Roll 34, documents 236 and 334.
38. *Nor'Wester*, May 1, 1869.
39. Secretary of Treasury to Lemay, Apr. 10, 1869, U.S. National Archives, document 261.
40. Ibid., Mar. 29, 1869, document 236.
41. Secretary of Treasury to Stoever, May 4, 1869, U.S. National Archives, document 334, lists L. Nutting as special agent.
42. Stutsman to Burleigh, Mar. 10, 1866, Faulk Papers, *Dakota Territorial Records*, Reel 43.
43. Stutsman to Faulk, Oct. 1, 1866, Faulk Papers, Reel 42.
44. Ibid.
45. Lamar, *Dakota Territory 1861–1889*, pp.95 and 112.
46. Stutsman to Faulk, Oct. 5, 1866, Faulk Papers, Reel 42.
47. Stutsman to Faulk, Oct. 11, 1866, Faulk Papers, Reel 42. Stutsman explained in the letter that the sparse turnout of the voters was attributable to the absence of most Métis on the fall buffalo hunt.
48. Lamar, *Dakota Territory 1861–1889*, p.112, n.40.
49. Stutsman to Sargent, Mar. 18, 1867, *Customs Records*, R.G. 36.
50. Armstrong, *Early Empire Builders*, p.53, states that Stutsman was unopposed. However, he also states, incorrectly, that it was to the *Council* that he was elected.
51. *Union and Dakotian*, Dec. 7, 1867.
52. Ibid.
53. Stutsman to Faulk, Sept. 28, 1868, Faulk Papers, Reel 42.
54. *House Journal*, 7th Session, Legislative Assembly, Dakota Territory, 1867–68, p.4. A concluding sentence is omitted.
55. *Union and Dakotian*, Jan. 11, 1868.
56. Faulk to Stutsman, Jan. 6, 1868, Faulk Papers, Reel 42.
57. Stutsman to Faulk, Jan. 6, 1868, Faulk Papers, Reel 42.
58. Addendum to Faulk letter, Jan. 6, 1868, Faulk Papers, Reel 42.
59. *House Journal*, pp.103–23.
60. *Council Journal*, Dakota Territory, 1867–68, pp.293–97.
61. *Union and Dakotian*, Jan. 11, 1868.
62. Stutsman to Faulk, Sept. 28, 1868, Faulk Papers, Reel 42.
63. Ibid.
64. Stutsman to Faulk, Oct. 9, 1868, Faulk Papers, Reel 42.
65. *Union and Dakotian*, Nov. 14, 1868.
66. Stutsman to Sargent, Oct. 15, 1868, *Customs Records*, R.G. 36.
67. *Union and Dakotian*, Oct. 31, 1868.
68. Stutsman to Faulk, Oct. 1, 1866, Faulk Papers, Reel 42.
69. Stutsman to Burleigh, March 31, 1869, Faulk Papers, Reel 42.
70. Lamar, *Dakota Territory 1861–1889*, p.117.

Notes

71. *Union and Dakotian*, Dec. 12, 1868.
72. Ibid., Dec. 19, 1868.
73. Ibid., Dec. 26, 1868.
74. Ibid., Jan. 2, 1869.
75. Pickler, "Excerpts from Correspondence," *South Dakota Historical Collections*, II (1904), pp.27–28.
76. Ibid.
77. Ibid.
78. Stutsman to Faulk, Sept. 28, 1868, Faulk Papers, Reel 42.
79. *Nor'Wester*, Sept. 29, 1868.

CHAPTER FOUR

1. See: D. Gibson and L. Gibson, *Substantial Justice* (1971), ch.I.
2. R.B. Hill, *Manitoba: The History of its Early Settlement, Development and Resources* (1890), p.182.
3. This description of the incident was taken primarily from the *Nor'Wester*, Sept. 29, 1868, supplemented by Hill, *Manitoba*, and A.C. Garrioch, *First Furrows* (1923), pp.172–73.
4. Council of Assiniboia Minutes, Aug. 6, 1868; E.H. Oliver, *The Canadian North-West: Its Early Development and Legislative Records* (1914), vol. I, p.587.
5. *Nor'Wester*, Sept. 29, 1868.
6. *Union and Dakotian*, Dec. 4, 1866.
7. Ibid., Dec. 14, 1867.
8. *Nor'Wester*, Sept. 29, 1868; Quarterly Court of Assiniboia Minutes, Sept. 25, 1868, Provincial Archives of Manitoba.
9. See: Gibson and Gibson, *Substantial Justice*, p.27ff.
10. See: R. St. G. Stubbs, *Four Recorders of Rupert's Land* (1967), p.135ff.
11. *Nor'Wester*, Sept. 29, 1868. The following description of the trial is from the same source except where otherwise indicated.
12. This and all subsequent quotations from the trial have been altered slightly from the third-person style of the newspaper report to the pronoun usage that a spectator would actually have heard.
13. J.F. Archbold, *Pleading and Evidence in Criminal Cases* (1867); *R. v. Holden* (1838) 8 C. & P. 606; *R. v. Stroner* (1845) 1 C. & P. 650; J.P. Bishop, *Criminal Procedure* (1880), p.588.
14. This third line of defence does not emerge clearly from the newspaper account, but is very likely to have been expressed in such terms.
15. Stutsman to Faulk, Sept. 28, 1868, Faulk Papers, Reel 42.
16. See the accounts of Hill, *Manitoba*, and Garrioch, *First Furrows*, for example.
17. *Nor'Wester*, Feb. 19, 1869.
18. Hill, *Manitoba*, p.185.
19. Frank L. Hunt, who had given up a law practice in Detroit to farm in Rupert's Land, had assisted in a celebrated abortion trial in 1863. (R. St.G. Stubbs, *Four Recorders of Rupert's Land*, p.147ff.) The chief advocate in that case had, however, been James Ross, who pleaded before the Rupert's Land courts on several occasions, and was eventually admitted to the Manitoba legal profession, but does not appear to have completed formal training as a lawyer.
20. "The Special Court," *Nor'Wester*, Sept. 29, 1868.

21. Charles Garratt, *Nor'Wester*, Feb. 12, 1869.
22. *Nor'Wester*, Oct. 17, 1868.
23. *Nor'Wester*, Sept. 29, 1868.
24. See: Gibson and Gibson, *Substantial Justice*, p.2ff.
25. Stutsman to Faulk, Sept. 28, 1868, Faulk Papers, Reel 42.

CHAPTER FIVE

1. *Report of Select Committee on the Hudson's Bay Company* (1857).
2. *Nor'Wester*, July 31, 1868.
3. See, for example: *Nor'Wester* editorials, Sept. 29, Oct. 10 and Oct. 17, 1868.
4. See letters from Charles Garratt, *Nor'Wester* Feb. 5 and Feb. 12, 1869.
5. *Nor'Wester*, Feb. 5, 1869.
6. *James Wickes Taylor Correspondence*, Minnesota Historical Society, Provincial Archives of Manitoba, M.G.5, B2, M233.
7. St. Paul *Daily Times*, Sept. 22, 1861.
8. *Nor'Wester*, Oct. 1, 1860.
9. Ibid., Sept. 28, 1860.
10. R.E. Sandborn, "The United States and the British North-West, 1865-70," *North Dakota Historical Quarterly*, Oct., 1931, pp.13-14; *Congressional Globe*, 39:1, p.3548.
11. J.B. Brebner, *North Atlantic Triangle: The Interplay of Canada, the United States and Great Britain* (1943), p.65.
12. St. Paul *Daily Press*, Feb. 27, 1868; U.S. National Archives, *Red River Dispatches*, T23; *Congressional Globe*, 40:2, p.2227.
13. Quoted in Sandborn, "United States and British North-West," pp.14-15.
14. Ramsey to Seward, Feb. 3, 1869, U.S. National Archives, *Miscellaneous Letters to Dept. of State*, 10-17-5, M179, Roll 295.
15. Ibid., Feb. 27, 1869.
16. Washburne to Ramsey, Mar. 15, 1869, U.S. National Archives, *Domestic Letters of Dept. of State, 1784-1906*, M40, Roll 65.
17. *Nor'Wester*, Oct. 10, 1868.
18. Stutsman to Faulk, Sept. 28, 1868, Faulk Papers, Reel 42.
19. See letters from "Liberty" and "Pemmican" to St. Paul *Daily Press*, Nov. 28, 1869 and Dec. 1, 1869.
20. Schultz to I.F. McDougall, Apr. 23, 1869, quoted in Stanley, *Louis Riel*, p.55.
21. Much has been written about Riel and the Riel Rebellion, but the most thorough study remains Stanley, *Louis Riel*, upon which this chapter draws heavily for background information.
22. Howard, *Strange Empire of Louis Riel*, p.104, appears to be the only historian to have mentioned Stutsman's role at this early stage, but the inferential evidence is strong.
23. McDougall to Howe, Oct. 31, 1869, Parliament of Canada, *Correspondence and Papers Connected with Recent Occurrences in the North-West Territories*, Ottawa (1870), p.6.
24. McDougall to Macdonald, Oct. 31, 1869, *Macdonald Papers*, Public Archives of Canada, M.G.26A, p.40751.
25. McDougall to Howe, Oct. 31, 1869, *Recent Occurrences* p.6.
26. McDougall to Howe, Nov. 5, 1869, *Recent Occurrences*, p.17.
27. Referred to by McDougall: McDougall to Howe, Nov. 29, 1869, *Recent Occurrences*, p.66.

28. Ibid.
29. Morton (ed.), *Journal of Alexander Begg*, p.180, Nov. 22, 1869. Begg states in his *History of the North-West*, vol. I (1894), p.404, that the document was "drawn up" by Stutsman. A letter from "Spectator" (one of Stutsman's pen-names), dated Dec. 6, 1869, and printed in the St. Paul *Daily Press* Dec. 18, 1869, asserts that it was "through the influence of the present heads of the provisional government" (the Riel forces), that the "Indians were induced to stand back and take no part whatever in the political troubles that might arise unless unjust coercion should be attempted."
30. Referred to in McDougall to Howe, Nov. 29, 1869, *Recent Occurrences*, p.66.
31. "Spectator" to St. Paul *Daily Press*, Nov. 1, 1869, published Nov. 14, 1869.
32. Five desired guarantees were mentioned in the letter, all of which later turned up, in very similar language, among the thirteen rights demanded in the List of Rights of December 1. (McDougall to Howe, Dec. 6, 1869, *Recent Occurrences*, p.6) See text page 120.
33. McDougall to Howe, Nov. 5, 1869, *Recent Occurrences*, p.17ff.
34. Ibid.
35. "Pembina" to St. Paul *Daily Press*, Nov. 3, 1869, published Nov. 15, 1869.
36. "Spectator" to St. Paul *Daily Press*, Nov. 4, 1869, published Nov. 15, 1869.
37. Willson, *Life of Lord Strathcona and Mount Royal*, p.291. The source is not cited, and a search of the U.S. National Archives and Library of Congress by the present writer in 1980 failed to produce the letter. There are also two internal oddities which cast some doubt on the authenticity of the document: Stutsman's name is misspelled, and the reference to his being an "official" does not appear to have been correct at this stage of his career. These discrepancies could have other explanations, however, The letter is certainly in the Stutsman style, and such a communication is a tactic that might well be expected of him.
38. W.R. Marshall to Grant, Nov. 22, 1869, *Miscellaneous Letters*, Roll 313.
39. McDougall to Howe, Nov. 4, 1869, *Recent Occurrences*, p.15.
40. Ibid., Nov. 5, 1869, p.17ff.
41. McDougall to Howe, Nov. 5, 1869, *Recent Occurrences*, p.17ff; and McDougall to Macdonald, *Macdonald Papers*, p.40779.
42. McDougall to Howe, Nov. 7, 1869, *Recent Occurrences*, p.22.
43. "Liberty" to St. Paul *Daily Press*, Dec. 5, 1869, published Dec. 6, 1869.
44. Sir Charles Tupper, *Recollections of Sixty Years* (1914), p.105.
45. McDougall to Howe, Dec. 8, 1869, *Recent Occurrences*, p.86ff.
46. Ibid., Nov. 5, 1869, p.17ff.
47. Ibid., Nov. 13, 1869, p.37ff.
48. McDougall to Howe, Nov. 13, 1869, *Recent Occurrences*, p.37ff; and Nov. 29, 1869, p.33.
49. McDougall to Howe, Nov. 5, 1869, *Recent Occurrences*, p.17ff; and Dec. 6, 1869, p.75ff.
50. McDougall requested government payment for Wallace's services for the period Nov. 1, 1869 to Jan. 7, 1870: McDougall to Macdonald, *Macdonald Papers*, M.G. 27I, C6, vol. 1, p.160, although there is evidence that he was suspected by the Métis before January. According to a letter from "Liberty" (Joseph Lemay) to the St. Paul *Daily Press*, Dec. 9, 1869, published Dec. 21, 1869, Wallace was arrested for spying that day.
51. McDougall to Macdonald, Nov. 8, 1869, *Macdonald Papers*, M.G. 27I, C6, vol. 1, p.40779.
52. McDougall to Macdonald, Nov. 18, 1869, *Macdonald Papers*, M.G. 27I, C6, vol. 1, p.40804.
53. Morton, *Journal of Alexander Begg*, pp.176–77, Nov. 22, 1869.
54. "Spectator" to St. Paul *Daily Press*, Nov. 8, 1869, published Nov. 21, 1869.

55. Morton, *Journal of Alexander Begg*, pp.176–77, Nov. 22, 1869.
56. The word used is "fit," but it is an obvious error.
57. Morton, *Journal of Alexander Begg*, pp.176–77, Nov. 22, 1869.
58. E.g.: "Spectator" to St. Paul *Daily Press*, Dec. 6, 1869, published Dec. 18, 1869.
59. Morton, *Journal of Alexander Begg*, p.242, Nov. 27, 1869.
60. Ibid., p.192, Nov. 30, 1869.
61. Stanley, *Louis Riel*, p.70.
62. Ibid., pp.71–72. Stanley does not mention Stutsman expressly.
63. Riel's notes of the Fort Garry convention, quoted in Stanley, *Louis Riel* p.73.
64. Ibid., pp.73–74.
65. Compare: "Spectator" to St. Paul *Daily Press*, Nov. 1, 1869, with Riel's List of Rights, McDougall to Howe, Dec. 6, 1869, *Recent Occurrences*, p.6.
66. Ibid., item 2, List of Rights.
67. Ibid., item 13.
68. Stanley, *Louis Riel*, p.74.
69. Ibid., p.75.
70. "Spectator" to St. Paul *Daily Press*, Dec. 4, 1869, published Dec. 21, 1869.
71. McDougall to Howe, Dec. 6, 1869, *Recent Occurrences*, p.79.
72. Dennis to McDougall, Dec. 2, 1869, *Recent Occurrences*, p.78.
73. McDougall to Howe, Dec. 6, 1869, *Recent Occurrences*, p.76.
74. Ibid.
75. Stanley, *Louis Riel*, p.75.
76. Interview with McDougall in St. Paul *Pioneer*, Jan. 4, 1870.
77. "S." to St. Paul *Daily Press*, Dec. 13, 1869, published Dec. 25, 1869.
78. Morton in *Journal of Alexander Begg*, p.76.
79. Diary of James Ross, Dec. 10, 1869, *Ross Papers*, Provincial Archives of Manitoba, #500.
80. McDougall to Howe, Dec. 2, 1869, *Recent Occurrences*, p.69ff.
81. Ibid.
82. "Spectator" to St. Paul *Daily Press*, Dec. 6, 1869, published Dec. 18, 1869.
83. McDougall to Howe, Dec. 8, 1869, *Recent Occurrences*, p.83ff; "Liberty" (Lemay) to St. Paul *Daily Press*, Dec. 7, 1869, published Dec. 21, 1869.
84. "Liberty" (Lemay) to St. Paul *Daily Press*, Dec. 7, 1869, published Dec. 21, 1869. McDougall's version was slightly different: "If the Indians take part in the war your life will not be safe for five minutes" (McDougall to Nelson, Dec. 8, 1869, *Recent Occurrences*, p.86ff.)
85. McDougall to Howe, Dec. 8, 1869, *Recent Occurrences*, p.83ff.
86. Ibid.
87. E.g.: Morton in *Journal of Alexander Begg*, p.87. An undated letter from Stutsman, using the pseudonym "E.", to the St. Paul *Daily Press*, published Jan. 5, 1870, expresses his concern that the appeal for military assistance "will be construed into a selfish desire for the establishment of a military post on this frontier."
88. "Liberty" to St. Paul *Daily Press*, Dec. 9, 1869, published Dec. 21, 1869.
89. Proclamation of Lieutenant and Conservator of the Peace in and for the North-West Territories, Dec. 9, 1869, quoted in St. Paul *Daily Press*, Dec. 25, 1869.
90. "Red River" to St. Paul *Daily Press*, Dec. 13, 1869, published Dec. 25, 1869.
91. Macdonald to McDougall, Nov. 27, 1869, quoted in Stanley, *Louis Riel*, p.76.

Notes

92. *McDougall to Riel, Dec. 13, 1869, Howe Papers,* Public Archives of Canada, M.G. 24 B29, vol. 31, p.205.
93. "E." to St. Paul *Daily Press,* undated, published Jan. 5, 1870. According to an unsigned letter to the same newspaper, Dec. 19, 1869, published Jan. 1, 1870, Richards' words were, "We will get even with you."
94. St. Paul *Pioneer,* Jan. 4, 1870.
95. W. MacDougall (sic), *The Red River Rebellion: Eight Letters to Hon. Joseph Howe* (1870), pp.5–6.
96. Begg notes, on Dec. 20, 1869, the receipt of a letter from Stutsman requesting material "for the use of Washington papers." (Morton, *Journal of Alexander Begg,* p.235.)
97. St. Paul *Daily Press,* Dec. 15, 1869, reporting events of Dec. 8.
98. Morton, *Journal of Alexander Begg,* p.234, Dec. 20, 1869.
99. Stutsman to Begg, Dec. 14, 1869, recorded in Morton, *Journal of Alexander Begg,* p.231, Dec. 16, 1869.
100. "Liberty" to St. Paul *Daily Press,* Dec. 6, 1869, published Dec. 18, 1869.
101. See: "Notebook of James Ross," in Morton, *Journal of Alexander Begg,* p.443: "Thursday, 9 Dec.... Went to Robert Taits' with my answer to Stutsman written at his request."
102. Stutsman to Riel, Dec. 25, 1869, recorded in Morton, *Journal of Alexander Begg,* p.240
103. Ibid.
104. The following account is drawn from Tupper, *Recollections of Sixty Years,* pp.101ff.
105. Ibid., p.116.
106. Morton, *Journal of Alexander Begg,* p.236, Dec. 22, 1869.
107. Rev. Dugast to Bishop Taché, Dec. 24, 1869, Archives of Archbishop of St. Boniface, T 7005.
108. Morton, *Journal of Alexander Begg,* p.240, Dec. 26, 1869.
109. Ibid., p.244, Dec. 28, 1869.
110. Ibid.
111. Ibid., p.246, Dec. 29, 1869.
112. *New Nation,* Jan. 7, 1870.
113. Morton, *Journal of Alexander Begg,* p.258, Jan. 11, 1870.
114. *New Nation,* Jan. 7 and Jan. 14, 1870.
115. Morton, *Journal of Alexander Begg,* p.259, Jan. 12, 1870.
116. Ibid., Jan. 13, 1870.
117. *Sioux City Daily Times,* Jan. 15, 1870.
118. *Union and Dakotian,* Feb. 17, 1870.
119. *Pioneer,* Jan. 21, 1870.
120. Taylor to Hamilton Fish, Feb. 2, 1870, U.S. National Archives, *Red River Dispatches,* T23.
121. Morton, *Journal of Alexander Begg,* p.259, Jan 12, 1870.
122. Ibid., p.253, Jan. 6, 1870.
123. Ibid., p.256, Jan. 9, 1870.
124. Ibid., p.259, Jan. 13, 1870.
125. Ibid., p.257, Jan. 10, 1870.
126. Stutsman to Riel, Jan. 11, 1870, *Riel Papers,* Provincial Archives of Manitoba, #20.
127. Morton, *Journal of Alexander Begg,* p.259, Jan. 13, 1870.
128. Ibid., p.261, Jan. 14, 1870.
129. Ibid., pp.285-87, Jan. 26, 1870.
130. Ibid., pp.253-254, Jan. 7, 1870.

131. Ibid., pp.260-61, Jan. 14, 1870.
132. Stutsman to Riel, Jan. 20, 1870, *Riel Papers*, Provincial Archives of Manitoba #21.
133. Begg, *History of the North-West*, p.441.
134. Morton, *Journal of Alexander Begg*, pp.292-93, Jan. 31, 1870.
135. Ibid., pp.287-90, Jan. 27, 1870.
136. Ibid., pp.165-70, Nov. 16, 1869.
137. Nelson to Dept. of State, Feb. 24, 1870, *Miscellaneous Letters*, Roll 319.
138. See: Morton, *Journal of Alexander Begg*, p.277ff, Jan. 21, Jan. 29, Feb. 19, Mar. 19 and Apr. 2, 1870.
139. Provencher to Tupper, Jan. 24, 1870, *Tupper Papers*, Public Archives of Canada, M.G. 26, F1(a), Vol. 3, p.1387; Lemay to Tupper, Feb. 14, 1870, *Tupper Papers*, p.1411.
140. St. Paul *Pioneer*, Feb. 16, 1870, printing an unsigned letter dated Feb. 1, 1870. The newspaper headline reads, in part: "Evil Effects of the Rolette-Stutsman Conspiracy."
141. E.g.: St. Paul *Daily Press*, Feb. 8, 1870.
142. Ibid., Jan. 15, 1870.
143. Malmros to Ramsey, Jan. 6, 1870, Minnesota Historical Society, *Ramsey Papers*, M203, Roll 19.
144. Malmros to Ramsey, Jan. 14, 1870, *Ramsey Papers*, Roll 19.
145. *Ramsey Papers*, Roll 40, Diary, Jan. 15, 1870.
146. St. Paul *Daily Press*, Feb. 8, 1870.
147. Ibid.
148. Malmros to Ramsey, *Ramsey Papers*, Roll 19.
149. Taylor to Fish, Feb. 2, 1870, *Red River Dispatches*, T23.
150. *Senate Executive Document #35*, 41st Congress, 2nd Session.
151. Malmros to Ramsey, Mar. 15, 1870, *Ramsey Papers*, Roll 19.
152. Ibid.
153. Enclosed in a letter, May 10, 1870, from the Deputy U.S. Consul in Winnipeg, Henry Robinson, to Davis: U.S. National Archives, *Diplomatic Dispatches from Winnipeg*, T24 (10-9-5), Roll 1 (emphasis added).
154. Boutwell to Fish, May 25, 1870, *Miscellaneous Letters*, Roll 325.
155. The British Legation in Washington had advised the Department of State about the pending expedition nine days previously: Thornton to Davis, May 16, 1870, U.S. National Archives, *Notes from British Legation to Dept. of State, 1791-1906*, M50, Roll 89.
156. Stevens to Ramsey, May 5, 1870, *Miscellaneous Letters*, Roll 324.
157. E.g.: Stevens to Ramsey, May 5, 1870, *Miscellaneous Letters*, Roll 324; Langford to Taylor, July 10, 1870, *Taylor Correspondence*, M.G. 5, B2, M233.
158. Langford to Taylor, July 10, 1870, *Taylor Correspondence*, M.G. 5., B2, M233.
159. Howard, *Strange Empire*, p.81.
160. Taylor to Ramsey, Nov. 15, 1870, *Ramsey Papers*, Roll 19, frames 526–28.
161. Stutsman to Faulk, June 6, 1870, Faulk Papers, Reel 43.

CHAPTER SIX

1. *Sioux City Daily Times*, July 8, 1870.
2. *Yankton Press*, vol. 1, no.1, Aug. 10, 1870.
3. Anonymous letter from Winnipeg to U.S. Department of State, Aug. 27, 1870, *Miscellaneous Letters*, Roll 332.

Notes

4. Stanley, *Louis Riel,* p.160.
5. *Manitoba News Letter,* Winnipeg, Sept. 13, 1870.
6. Stanley, *Louis Riel,* p.163; Stanley, "Riel's Petition to the President of the United States, 1870," *Canadian Historical Review,* Dec. 1939, p.427.
7. Howard, *Strange Empire* p.189.
8. *Bismarck Daily Trubune,* Dec. 28, 1887.
9. Stutsman to Faulk, June 6, 1870, Faulk Papers, Reel 43.
10. Register of Deeds, Cavalier, North Dakota, *Record Book A, Pembina County, 1868–1880,* Transactions A16 and A23.
11. Crowell to Ramsey, Oct. 27, 1870, *Ramsey Papers,* documents 52Off.
12. *U.S. Census Roll,* 1870, Pembina Territory and Town of Pembina, p.21. Stutsman's age is listed as 40 (he was actually 44), which may indicate that he was willing to modify reality in the interests of vanity. It is possible that he also underestimated his worth for some reason, but exaggeration of it would have been more in character. In any event, the estimate of $150,000 was wholly unreasonable; there had been no opportunity during his career to earn such a huge sum. It should be remembered, also, that most of his wealth was in the form of slow-selling Yankton real estate. It is interesting to note, however, that Stutsman reported a much higher personal worth than anyone else in the area.
13. *Record Book A, Pembina County,* Transactions A25 & A62. See also Stutsman's will, Jan. 22, 1874, State Historical Society of North Dakota, Bismarck, which indicates no property in the Pembina area other than that which *Record Book A* shows to have been purchased from the three persons named.
14. *Union and Dakotian,* Oct. 29, 1870.
15. H.V. Arnold, *History of Old Pembina, 1780-1872* (1917), pp.158-59.
16. *Yankton Press,* Oct. 4, 1871, letter of denial from Court Clerk George I. Foster.
17. Ibid., Nov. 29, 1871.
18. Stutsman to Batchelor, Sept. 23, 1871, Dakota Territorial Records, *Correspondence of Territorial Secretary,* Reel 48.
19. Lemay to Taché, Mar. 12, 1870, Archives of Archbishop of St. Boniface.
20. Stanley, *Louis Riel,* pp.169-76.
21. Stoever to Taylor, Oct. 8, 1871, *Taylor Correspondence,* MG5, B2, Reel 2, M233.
22. Archibald to Taylor, Oct. 10, 1871, *Taylor Correspondence,* MG5, B2, Reel 2, M233.
23. *Yankton Press,* Nov. 8, 1871; Wheaton to Taylor, Oct. 21, 1871, *Taylor Correspondence,* MG5, B2, Reel 2, M233.
24. Bain to Mair, Oct. 21, 1871, *Mair Papers,* Queen's University Archives, Series I, Correspondence Box I, Folder 2.
25. Stutsman to Taylor, March 11, 1872, *Taylor Correspondence,* MG5, B2, Reel 2, M233.
26. Ramsey to Fish, Dec. 24, 1871, *Miscellaneous Letters* Roll 361.
27. *Record Book A, Pembina County,* Transaction A59, Mar. 2, 1872.
28. *Record Book A, Pembina County,* Transactions A62, A64, A66, A68, A70, A72, A74, & A76, Mar. 4, 1872.
29. E.g.: conveyance from Stutsman to Hancock, Dec. 27, 1873, *Record Book A, Pembina County,* Transaction 276, in which almost an entire block was transferred for an expressed consideration of $5.00.
30. C.A. Loundsberry, *Early History of North Dakota* (1919), pp.496 and 529.
31. Kingsbury, *History of Dakota Territory.*

32. *Bismarck Daily Tribune*, Dec. 28, 1887.
33. *Dakota Herald*, Feb. 3, 1874.
34. *Yankton Press and Dakotian*, Feb. 5, 1874.
35. Stutsman will, Jan. 22, 1874, State Historical Society of North Dakota. A copy of the will is appended to Marjorie Stoa's Master's thesis, *Enos Stutsman: Influential Pioneer*, p.85. Probate is noted in *Record Book A, Pembina County*, Feb. 28, May 15, and June 2, 1874.
36. The *Grantor Index of Deeds, A, Pembina County*, pp.239–45 and 253, shows a total price of $17,700, but since his cash was bequeathed to the Cavaliers, the transaction appears to have been a formality.
37. Kingsbury, "Enos Stutsman", p.353.

INDEX

177

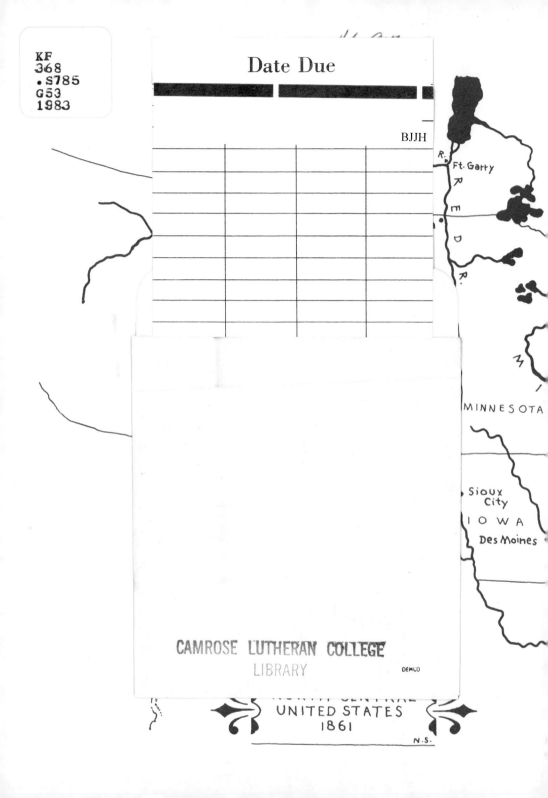

Date Due

BJJH

Ft. Garty

MINNESOTA

Sioux
City

IOWA

Des Moines

UNITED STATES
1861

N.S.